East African Hip Hop

**INTERPRETATIONS OF CULTURE
IN THE NEW MILLENNIUM**

A list of books in the series appears at the end of the book.

East African Hip Hop

Youth Culture and Globalization

MWENDA NTARANGWI

UNIVERSITY OF ILLINOIS PRESS

Urbana and Chicago

Library of Congress Cataloging-in-Publication Data
Ntarangwi, Mwenda.
East African hip hop: youth culture and globalization /
Mwenda Ntarangwi.
p.   cm. — (Interpretations of culture in the new millennium)
Includes bibliographical references and index.
ISBN 978-0-252-03457-2 (cloth : alk. paper) —
ISBN 978-0-252-07653-4 (pbk. : alk. paper)
1. Youth—Africa, East—Social conditions.
2. Group identity—Africa, East. 3. Hip-hop—Africa, East.
4. Adolescent psychology—Africa, East. 5. Blacks—Race
identity—Africa, East. 6. Popular culture and globalization—
Africa, East. 7. Music and globalization—Africa, East.
8. Africa, East—Social life and customs. I. Title.
HQ799.A353N78   2009
305.23509676'09049—dc22   2009009436

Contents

Preface

Contemporary globalization has intensified competition and growth in economic and knowledge networks across community and national boundaries, internationalized markets and diminished the role of the state in economic matters, and increased networks and exchanges of people and knowledge. Despite undeniable changes brought by globalization, scholars show that various individuals, communities, and nations have experienced its effects differently. There have also been varied responses to globalization across time and space. This reality leads to a number of questions pursued in this book: How has globalization shaped collective and individual lives in East Africa? What is the relationship between youth and globalization in the context of a fast-changing political and economic landscape in East Africa? How have youth taken advantage of globalization despite its dual role as a process that is both constraining and liberating?

Taking globalization as a process that interacts with the local in complex and dynamic ways, hip hop music is used in the current volume as an analytical tool to respond to these and other related questions, including how East African youth encounter and make sense of lived and imagined experiences within global economic and political structures. Almost always, youth in East Africa use hip hop to create spaces through which they enter a public domain that often excludes them in favor of those who wield social, political, and economic power. In this way, globalization is, on the one hand, a force that replicates unequal structural, economic, and political relations that the West has had with Africa and, on the other, a force that creates opportunities for youth to enter into the public space, make some economic gains, and offer sociocultural critique. Hip hop also is a force that the youth use to position themselves in an ever-changing and challenging world.

Research for the current volume straddles many years cumulatively comprising three years of fieldwork in three East African nations—Kenya, Uganda, and Tanzania. Data were collected through interviews with various artistes, observations and participation in live shows, and use of secondary resources such as books, magazines, radio shows, and the World Wide Web. I collected, transcribed, and translated 143 songs, many of which are used in this work. Even when collecting data from these different geographic spaces, I often encountered what has become almost a standard challenge to many contemporary ethnographic projects—the changing nature of the location of the field site. As argued elsewhere (Ntarangwi 2003c), studying music has compelled me to expand my notions of the "field" to include fluid and flexible locations and productions of place. Gottlieb and Graham accurately show this trend in ethnography.

> [M]any in our discipline are pushing the conceptual limits of the very notion of an appropriate field site or community, expanding its classic locus in non-Western villages to factories, urban elites, ethnographers' native communities, novels, science and the scientific laboratory, the Internet, the telephone, the theater, transnational sites, multiple sites, and so on. (Gottlieb and Graham 1999, 118–19)

My experiences in the three East African countries often included unrecognizable borders, as the music and the artistes crossed national, cultural, and generational boundaries with ease. The transnational nature of hip hop music makes the classic spatial location of a research site in one bounded territory untenable. Yet, this was not the only epistemological and methodological challenge I faced. In writing this book was the challenge of categorization and definition. Even though the term hip hop here denotes the genre of music analyzed, it is a term born of compromise rather than a reflection of a specific and easily defined musical tradition. In this book, the term *hip hop* refers to the popular music in East Africa that emerged, in different phases and forms, at the end of the 1980s and that broke ranks with erstwhile traditional or local styles associated with regions or ethnic groups such as *benga, muziki wa dansi,* or *cavacha,* which would be the preferred focus of a classic ethnomusicological study (e.g., Barz 2004). Hip hop in this sense combines elements of local, popular musical traditions with mostly American (U.S.) and Jamaican music styles of rap and raga, respectively. It also reflects the local contestations of what defines East African youth's music of the last decade, which has been referred to as *muziki wa kizazi kipya* (music of a new generation) and *muziki wa vijana* (music of the youth).

In Arusha (a Tanzanian town locally known by artistes as A-Town), for instance, a number of musicians including the well-known group Xplastaz, consider their music "true" hip hop because of the lyrical focus on tough social and political realities of the day as opposed to their Dar es Salaam counterparts (especially those referred to as the East Coast group) who perform *bongo flava,* a form of hip hop whose lyrics glorify self and extol bling bling. In Kenya, a similar scenario emerges with some critics seeing contemporary popular music such as *kapuka* (associated with Ogopa DJs) and *genge* (popularized by the artiste Nonini) that are a result of a blend of hip hop, dance hall, and traditional music styles as music with very little social relevance beyond entertainment. This style of music, as some musicians with whom I spoke in Kenya said, is unlike "real" hip hop performed by such groups as Ukooflani Mau Mau, Mtapa Risiki, and Muki Garang that focuses on the struggles of youth and other marginalized groups (see also Ferrari 2007). The Uganda music scene is a little different from that seen in Kenya and Tanzania as it has tended to be dominated by dancehall raga and R&B blended in with local styles. A few artistes such as Sylvester and Abramz and Krazy Native perform a style of hip hop locally referred to as Luga-flow, which seeks to connect lyrics with the everyday realities of the underclass and sung in Luganda. The most successful Ugandan artiste, Chameleone, performs a local version of raga with predominantly Swahili lyrics that also articulates the prevailing social problems. Yet, various artistes come together to compose and sing songs about social problems as was the case for Halima Namakula, Butcherman, and Ngoni Group, who collaborated in a song that highlighted the plight of internally displaced people in Gulu, Northern Uganda. Because my focus is on social issues and the reconstitution of youth agency through their music, I refer to this music as hip hop even though I am aware that some of the artistes included in my analysis may not locally be considered "real" hip hop artistes.

Chapter 1 places hip hop, agency, and globalization within larger scholarly discussions and writing in order to show how economic changes emanating from elsewhere shape the realities of lives experienced by many youth in East Africa by creating opportunities while also reinscribing dominance and exploitation. I reflect on the scholarship of music and hip hop in East Africa, showing the role of agency in understanding how one enters into the public sphere through a medium over which one has some degree of control.

Finally, the chapter highlights some of the methods used in gathering data for this work.

African identity is placed at the center of an analysis of the emergence of a hip hop culture in East Africa in chapter 2. Using various examples from hip hop song texts, this identity is discussed within the context of Africa's encounters with colonialism and imperialism and the emergent collective and individual notions of self and the Other. To understand the role played by youth in critiquing sociocultural and political realities in their nations, the chapter asks how Africans have been viewed and have viewed themselves within the cross-cultural encounter precipitated by the forces of colonialism, imperialism, and now globalization. As products of different political, economic, and cultural movements, (East) Africans embody a canvas on which to paint performance of hip hop with broad, colorful, and truncated strokes that highlight change, continuity, and even fragmentation in their individual and collective identities.

Chapter 3 expands on the notion of identity to include gender as an analytical framework that allows exploration and understanding of the power differentials and contested meanings of modernity that surround men's and women's lives. The chapter shows that while hip hop opens up spaces for young people to articulate lived and imagined experiences, such spaces are not equally accessed by both men and women. If anything, hip hop is used to reclaim conservative and essentialized notions of femininity and masculinity with many youth denouncing the blurred gender identity lines, such as hair styles, body piercing, and mode of dress, that accompany American hip hop and that are slowly emerging on the East African scene. These songs also broach the topic of sex and sexuality but, unlike many similar songs, they show the real consequences of reckless living and unprotected sex.

Chapter 4 is an exploration of the reality of economic hardships faced by many East Africans as they navigate the neoliberal, market-driven economic hegemony championed through privatization and the reduction of the role of the state in the provision of basic social services. These political and economic changes have expanded the gap between the poor and the rich, as have opportunities for exploitation and appropriation. I argue that many youth use hip hop to articulate their discontent with this economic arrangement while turning their wrath on their own leaders who have uncritically embraced these changes because they favor the elite and marginalize the poor.

Chapter 5 is an analysis of the role youth play in not only publicizing the discussion of the state of and stigma around HIV/AIDS but also of sex and sexuality in cultures where sex education is almost taboo in formal education. Shown are the responses made by some politicians, religious leaders, and other interest groups to hip hop's campaigns for the promotion of safe sex through distribution of condoms and HIV/AIDS testing. While the youth are embracing the need to publicly recognize and discuss sex and sexuality as a way of reducing new infections and responding to stigma around people with HIV/AIDS, much of the public, especially those in positions of power, as well as religious leaders, are, like the proverbial ostrich, burying their heads in the sand and avoiding an open discussion and confrontation with the issues. Finally, by highlighting the condom, for instance, hip hop has provided a lens through which to view East African notions, attitudes, and discussions of sex and sexuality.

Chapter 6 is the conclusion that recaptures the role hip hop plays in opening up critical terrains for understanding not only sociocultural realities in East Africa but also youth identities and African modernities in the twenty-first century. Rather than seeing hip hop as a completely new cultural phenomenon in East Africa, one is better off seeing it as a window into the culture of change in the East Africa's political, economic, and social realities created by local and global processes. Ending this section is a discussion of the struggles many youth in East Africa go through to legitimize hip hop as a bona fide form of cultural expression amid concerns of its signification of hooliganism and thuggism.

This ethnography of hip hop in East Africa emphasizes the role of youth in shaping their own experiences within a specific politico-economic epoch and as mediated through their performances. It is an important contribution to the understanding of hip hop as a cultural frame that helps those who are ethnographers and the youth who are the practitioners to understand the nature of the reality of the everyday lives of the youth and as a blueprint of how things ought to be conducted. This interpretation draws from Clifford Geertz's notion of culture as "models of" and "models for" experience (1973). It is a window into how the youth make sense of their own existence within a global context of inequality while projecting, through their own daily activities and performances, what that world ought to look like.

Acknowledgments

Research for this project started in the year 2000, but the bulk of it was generously supported by funds from the offices of the dean and president at Augustana College, Rock Island, Illinois, to whom I am most grateful. I am also indebted to Richard Shauri in Dar es Salaam, who was kind enough to link me up with many musicians. And thank you also to the numerous artistes in Dar es Salaam, including Professor Jay, Mkoloni, Kali P, Saidog, Sista P, Mheshimiwa Temba, Ras Lion, John Woka, and Zay B, and to Zakaria Mwita at Femina and Rebecca Arnold, who introduced me to a number of contacts in Dar es Salaam. To all of them, I say, "*Asante sana!*" I am grateful to Richard Ssewakiryanga and Moses Mbattide at the Center for Basic Research and to Jackie and Jack in Wandegeya, all of Uganda, and to Kang'ethe Ngigi, Felo, and Barbara in Kenya. I am also grateful to my colleagues at Augustana College, including Peter Kivisto, Tom Mayer, Adam Kaul, Meg Gillette, Dan Lee, Nirmala Salgado, and Pramod Mishra, who read and commented on various parts of this project. I am also greatly indebted to anonymous reviewers of the manuscript especially one whose meticulous reading and comments on the manuscript have truly shaped this final version. Norm E. Whitten Jr., professor emeritus, University of Illinois, and Joan Catapano at the University of Illinois Press have been extremely supportive, and their encouragement and honest and quick responses to my drafts of the manuscript mean a lot to me.

All the time and peace of mind necessary to complete this work were made possible by my wonderful family—my wife, Margaret, and our two lovely daughters, Nkatha and Gatwiri, who I pray will grow to be social advocates for the communities with whom they will be living. To all of you, thank you from the bottom of my heart.

East African Hip Hop

1

Globalization and
Youth Agency in East Africa

What do we gain through privatization?
We are tricked to embrace this privatization because
If you scrutinize carefully you will see that we are being ripped off
—Wagosi wa Kaya, "Tumeshtuka (We are shocked)"

These words by this Tanzanian group that comprises two artistes—
Mkoloni (Fred Mariki) and Dr. John (John Simba)—point to an important
component of globalization that has shaped the lives of East Africans in various ways. They pinpoint the process of privatization that has come to define
much of the economic globalization affecting many individuals, communities, and nations in East Africa and beyond. As Mkoloni once responded to
a question on what his thoughts were on globalization, "Globalization has
been there for a long time, it's only that people did not know what to call
it,"[1] which directly reflects what many scholars have said about the historical
roots of globalization (e.g., Amselle 2002; Cooper 2001). I told him that I
had noticed many young people selling all manner of wares including used
clothes, electronics, shoes, and fruit in his neighborhood in Sinza Madukani,
on the outskirts of Dar es Salaam, and that this was an indication that these
jobs were the fruits of globalization. He commented, "I disagree with you
on the issue of 'fruits of globalization' because those jobs are not consistent
and do not constitute legitimate work. The people working such jobs do not
pay taxes and are, therefore, not recognized by the government. That is why
they are harassed every day. Globalization gives them an opportunity and
then blocks them right there as they try to move forward."[2] This response
ties very well with what he and Dr. John state in the excerpted song above
about being "tricked to embrace" privatization that is "ripping them off."
They are articulating the double-edged nature of globalization by showing

the disparity between the stated benefits of globalization (Ajayi 2001; Rodrik 1997; Stiglitz 2003) and the practical realities of its (negative) effects.

This current study of globalization, hip hop, and youth agency takes a critical look at how globalization provides both opportunities and challenges for youth in East Africa through hip hop, a genre of music that is both a product of globalization as well as a medium to critique globalization. I argue that although contemporary globalization or what Marc Edelman and Angelique Haugerud call "a renewed era of globalization since 1980" (2005, 23) has increased connections among people, communities, and nations (Appadurai 1996; Lewellen 2002; Stiglitz 2003; Wolf 2004), it has also made clear the socioeconomic disparities among these individuals, communities, and nations it has connected. As a result, even as globalization has increased the ability to communicate across geographic and political boundaries and even made it easier to access goods and products from almost every corner of the world (for instance, cell phones and "ethnic" crafts that are widespread in the world today), some scholars say that there has not been any marked difference in economic growth worldwide between the beginning of the twentieth century and the beginning of the twenty-first century (e.g., Friedman 2005; Mkandawire 2002). It is quite telling that world trade in 2001, which is estimated at 31 percent of world output, is lower than the 33 percent attained in 1913 (Mkandawire 2002, 1).

In using the term *globalization,* I seek to capture this historical process of contact and even conquest across geographical, cultural, and political boundaries in which people, ideas, goods, and capital circulate over an expanded terrain and period. This approach to globalization follows that of many anthropologists who see it as signifying "accelerated flows or intensified connections—across national and other boundaries—of commodities, people symbols, technology, images, information, and capital, as well as disconnections, exclusions, marginalization, and disposition" (Edelman and Haugerud 2005, 2). It is an approach that is also cognizant of critiques that regard current notions of globalization as missing historical depth of interconnections (Amselle 2002; Cooper 2001) or even leaving out Africa altogether because of its inconvenience in fitting the "global convergence narratives" (Ferguson 2006, 28). In doing so, however, I am not denying the increased contact, exchange, and integration of previously isolated communities or economies (albeit in unequal terms) precipitated by contemporary globalization through flows of people, goods, capital, and ideas (see Giddens 2003; Kearney 1995; Lewellen 2002; Wolf 2004, among many others).

In Africa, the process of contemporary globalization has been mobilized by the promise of economic growth envisaged by such institutions as the World Bank (World Bank 1981, 1988, 1992, 2004) and reflected in the rapid economic and sociopolitical changes propelled by the intensification of foreign-derived notions of development and social change (Ferguson 2006; Macamo 2005). Globalization in Africa thus has its roots in the historical processes of contact and conquest especially in such overt structures as colonialism through which African economies were systematically entrenched in world economic systems (Edelman and Haugerud 2005) and in the neocolonial politicoeconomic project of the period between 1970s and early 1980s when the neoliberal economic agenda, pushed by the International Monetary Fund (IMF) and World Bank and articulated through the structural adjustment programs (SAPs), undermined and negatively affected African economic and political structures. These two processes (colonialism and neocolonialism) have shaped the current form of globalization that is discussed in the current book. The effects of colonialism and neocolonialism are entrenched in both individual and collective identities and activities and intimately interact with internal social, economic, and political structures. Through an analysis of hip hop and the ways it embodies all these processes, we have a forum for reflecting, critiquing, and even taking advantage of this contemporary form of globalization. Hip hop is then a forum through which East African youth, often left out of important socioeconomic and political commentaries and decision-making processes, attain agency that enables them to variably shape their lives and participate in raising public awareness and consciousness to social and political issues while also appropriating it for their own economic and political gain.

This book follows Sherry Ortner's use of the term *agency* to denote hip hop artiste's "intentionality and the pursuit of (culturally defined) projects . . . within relations of social inequality, asymmetry, and force" (2006, 139) that, in turn, creates for them what William Sewell calls a "capacity for desiring, for forming intentions and for acting creatively" (1992, 20) in their lives despite the social, political, and economic constraints brought by globalization. Using this definition will help to avoid falling into the trap of giving "precedence to individuals over contexts" and assume "that humans can triumph over their context through sheer force of will," as identified by Jean Comaroff and John Comaroff (1992, 10). Instead, I see youth agency through hip hop as a means of retaining autonomy and the ability to act on their own behalf while influencing other people in political discourse and even economic activity in spite of the global forces of inequality and exploitation that they face. To consider these issues in any other way would be to emphasize the complete lack of agency as some anthropologists tend to do when studying postcolonial communities and show "the degree to which colonialism [or globalization] so formed or deformed the societies in question that . . . [they now have] virtually no cultural authenticity at all" (Ortner 2006, 143). I reject that kind of approach and mobilize these two concepts of globalization and agency by using hip hop (itself a product of global flows) as a tool and a forum for shaping youth's subjective realities and as a form of gainful economic activity.

Globalization and Hip Hop in East Africa

Undoubtedly, many external factors as well as internal uncertainties and failures in economic and political management of individual African nations have all had enormous effects on local cultural and social structures (Aina 2004; Haugerud 1995; Mkandawire and Soludo 1999; Offiong 2001; Van Binsbergen 2004). Some results of these features and pressures have been the growth of pockets of globalization especially in urban areas where a few Africans with capital, knowledge, and social connections emerge as the new faces of globalization—able to travel across national and international boundaries with ease, consume and access global cultural products, and embodying what Arjun Appadurai refers to as the transformed "everyday subjectivities through electronic mediation and the work of imagination" (1996, 10). Many of these Africans constitute the elite in their communities and often travel far and wide, making economic transactions, increasing their knowledge bases, and acquiring new tastes for foreign goods and mannerisms (Shivji 2006), allowing them direct links and dialogue with worlds outside their geopolitical locales especially in the Western metropolis. Yet, it would be erroneous to limit these global flows to only the elite in Africa when they have also affected other members of these communities, especially the youth. As a result, the youth have variably "punctuated, interrogated, and domesticated . . . the megarhetoric of developmental modernization (economic growth, high technology, agribusiness, schooling, militarization) through the micronarratives of film, television, music, and other expressive forms which allow modernity to be rewritten as vernacular globalization" (Appadurai 1996, 10).

This "vernacularization" process of global flows and the expansion of neoliberal economic and political structures are critical in the analysis pursued in this work because the intense expansion of foreign-derived modes of socioeconomic development coincided with the emergence of a hip hop culture in East Africa especially among urban youth in the capital cities of Nairobi, Dar es Salaam, and Kampala in Kenya, Tanzania, and Uganda, respectively (see Perullo 2007; Ntarangwi 2007; and Ssewakiryanga 1999). These socioeconomic processes that produced hip hop in East Africa also mirrored those that produced U.S. hip hop in the Bronx (Kelley 2006) and other expressive forms such as "seditious" music in Kenya (Haugerud 1995), hip hop in Japan (Condry 2006), and "ghetto" music in Tanzania (Remes 1998), to give but a few examples. In this regard, a direct link can be seen between growing politicoeconomic constraints and the expansion of music as a forum for social critique.

In East Africa, for instance, these constraints are linked to the neoliberal economic project that opened up local markets to foreign (mostly Western) goods and cultural products such as movies, music, dress, and other opportunities for cultural exchange (or dominance) through satellite television, FM radio, e-mail, the Internet, cell phones, and other forms of cultural expression. This influx of foreign goods, ideas, and sensibilities into East Africa was set in motion by two major factors: first, the weakening of the nation-state following market fundamentalism propelled by conditionalities and fiscal austerity imposed by the IMF and World Bank through SAPs and, second, the diminishing of the role of the nation-state as a legitimate agent for socializing youth (Diouf 2003). In view of this fragility of the nation-state, popular participation or decent inclusion in sociopolitical decision making by the various nationals becomes negligible and slowly breeds a desire for alternative modes of governance and politicocultural expression.

The youth took advantage of this political fragility, especially through a combination of factors such as easy access to recording and dissemination of music (Perullo 2007), and embraced hip hop and its various facets for self-expression. Through hip hop the youth have been able to gradually insert themselves into the local and global spheres that shape national and regional political and cultural structures in unprecedented ways. Indeed, numerous opportunities availed to many youth in East Africa through hip hop have enabled a number of them to redefine their relations to the nation-state, to their communities, and their own social identities. These realities are not lost to hip hop musicians themselves, who frequently hail the new social and economic opportunities that have shaped their personal lives. Kenya's hip hop artist, Chiz 'n' Brain, credits Kenya's hip hop group, Ukooflani Mau Mau, for his ability to avoid a life of self-destruction. In a short biography about his career in music, Chiz 'n' Brain says, "Ukooflani has changed me. I would have been lost in alcoholism because I had nothing better to do. Day in day out, I was idle. Ukooflani gave me focus."[3] Similar sentiments were expressed by Professor Jay of Tanzania, who finds in hip hop his real calling, stating, "*Sasa ninaishi muziki* (Now I make a living through music)."[4] This positive view of youth and hip hop may differ with that expressed by others who often see youth in hip hop as vagabonds, misfits, and lazy persons.[5] These new reconstructions of the self are, however, not without sociopolitical challenges, especially when it comes to facing real-life issues that involve the police as is evident in the following narrative of an encounter in Dar es Salaam, Tanzania, during my final day of fieldwork in the summer of 2006.

A Caterpillar Tractor and a Ford Fiesta

On my last day in Dar es Salaam in the summer of 2006, my local research interlocutor—Richard Shauri, a hip hop artiste whose stage name is Rich One—offered to drive me to the airport to catch my 2:00 P.M. flight back to my "base" in Nairobi, Kenya. Rich owns a 1970s Ford Fiesta that he fondly refers to as the "Escalade." We had earlier agreed that instead of taking a cab to the airport, Rich would give me a ride in return for gas for the "Escalade." That was a good exchange because he had been very helpful in my research in Dar es Salaam. At exactly 11:00 A.M., Rich pulled up at my hotel; in the car were his girlfriend and a fellow musician whom I only know by his stage name, Saidog. I placed my carry-on bag in the tiny space in the trunk, between the back seat and the huge speaker that was belting out hip hop music, and sat in the front seat of the "Escalade." Rich had earlier told me that an American friend had given him the car as a gift. When he received it, the car had some few mechanical problems that Rich had to take care of, including finding an alternative set of drive shafts that required some creativity on the part of the mechanic. It was hard to get spare parts for such an old car in a region dominated by Japanese, German, and British vehicles. Furthermore, it is a left-hand-drive vehicle in a country where almost everyone else drives a right-hand-drive vehicle. Some mechanic in Arusha had, however, been able to fit some Nissan drive shafts into the "Escalade" with a little bit of mechanical persuasion that became quite detectable when the car was in motion. The car tended to wobble when it got up to a speed of forty miles per hour.

I placed my computer bag on my lap as we started our forty-five-minute drive to the airport. Other than the traffic that we encountered as we left downtown Dar es Salaam, the rest of the trip was smooth until fifteen minutes away from the airport. Rich noticed that the car was overheating and pulled into the closest Shell gas station to take a look. We opened the hood to see if the car was out of coolant. Upon loosening the radiator cap, a brownish, hot liquid started bubbling out, making it clear that the radiator was dirty and hot. We asked one of the gas station attendants if there was a mechanic on duty and he said there was none. We decided to cool down the radiator and then try to make the rest of the trip to the airport before I got late for my flight. Our makeshift cooling strategy of pouring cold water on the radiator seemed to work as the temperature gauge was slowly going down. I secretly checked my watch to make sure I had enough time to catch my flight. I had previously missed my flight from Nairobi to Dar es Salaam, which had forced me to spend an unplanned day and night in Nairobi, besides paying a change-of-reservation penalty.

When Rich was satisfied that the radiator was cool enough for us to use the car, he closed the hood and asked that we get into the car and proceed to the airport. He pulled behind a huge Caterpillar tractor that was also trying to rejoin the traffic into the road to the airport. The driver of the Caterpillar must have changed his mind or had grown impatient waiting for the other vehicles to allow him into the lane and decided to go the opposite direction from the airport. However, he was too close to the road and could not just turn and go left to avoid the traffic buildup. So he decided to back up. The tractor was so big and high that we could not see the driver, who must have been about four feet above us. I helplessly looked at this monster of a machine now approaching us with a beeping sound that seemed to get louder every second. Rich was unable to react quickly enough to back the car and avoid being crushed by the tractor. All he could do was blow his horn that did nothing to stop the monster of a tractor from coming at us. On the right-hand side of us, I saw a pedestrian waving at the Caterpillar driver trying to make him stop and pointing in our direction in a desperate attempt to alert him that there was a car behind his tractor.

The beeping sound of the tractor seemed like a death timer, growing louder and louder as the monster retreated towards our now-stationary vehicle. Then it dawned on me! We were about to be crushed. I said a short prayer and watched as the end of my life approached. I told myself that I had lived a good life but was sad that I had not seen my family in four months. What a way to die! I had seen in some movies how people who were about to be crushed opened car doors and ran to safety. I guess that only happens in movies because none of that seemed to be possible in the world I inhabited at the time. I did not have the thought or energy to open the door and get away from the approaching disaster. Neither could Rich. I looked at him from the corner of my left eye and saw his mouth wide open in a mix of shock and fear. The Caterpillar's steel bottom was now literally in my face with the car windshield as my only protection. The tires of the tractor were so big that the base of the tractor was actually higher than the top of our car's hood. It was clear that this monster needed only seconds to completely crush us.

Rich was speechless, just like everyone else in the car. As the Caterpillar kept coming, I heard the car's hood crunching like an empty soda can underneath a strong boot. I closed my eyes and waited to be crushed. Then the beeping stopped. After a few seconds that seemed like eternity, I slowly opened my eyes only to see a middle-aged man standing at Rich's window. I realized he was the driver of the Caterpillar tractor. He was yelling at Rich in Kiswahili, accusing him of crushing into his tractor. A crowd had already gathered around our car. I slowly reached for the door knob, opened it, and stepped out of the vehicle. The pedestrian who had earlier tried to stop the Caterpillar driver from crushing us said he had warned him but nobody seemed to take heed. I became aware of what was going on around me. The car engine was still running, and the music was still playing. Ironically the song that was playing at the time was "Tuko Freshi (We are fresh)" by Uk-ooflani Mau Mau, which was off a CD that I had given to Rich. The song had been playing throughout this ordeal and seemed ironically appropriate for the occasion. Part of the song's lyrics went like this:

> We can't be shocked
> neither are we scared
> We are fresh and hip
> so don't disrespect us!

The song must have meant something different to the composer than it did at this time with the Caterpillar tractor literally sitting on the tiny Ford Fiesta. The crowd gathering around us was getting bigger, and all kinds of theories were being spun to explain what was happening. Rich looked at me and asked, "*Mkubwa tufanye nini* (What do we do, sir?)." Honestly, I had no clue. I was in that moral-cultural-circumstantial situation that many anthropologists hope they never get caught up in. I was reminded of Alma Gottlieb and Philip Graham's dilemma as they watched a young Beng woman in Ivory Coast being forced to have sex with her husband-to-be as a way to subdue her into accepting an arranged marriage. This was happening in the watch of many members of the community, some of whom were helping pin her down. What could Alma and Philip do in this situation? They were baffled when the young woman's mother came out of the room cussing at her daughter for not accepting to go through the ordeal (Gottlieb and Graham 1994). I, like Alma and Philip, could only watch and hope that the people involved would solve the matter in locally appropriate ways.

While many East Africans clearly enjoy the products of American technological progress exemplified by the Caterpillar tractor and Ford car, they
are subject to local forms of justice tainted with corruption. I overheard the
Caterpillar driver on his cell phone say he had been hit by a small car from
the rear and was getting delayed. Although I had mixed feelings about Rich
getting justice, I could not believe the driver's version of the story. His tractor
was an inch away from crushing us to death, and now it was our fault! The
sad reality was that he was right.

In Tanzania, as it is in many other countries, if one has a motor-vehicle
accident, the vehicle in the rear is always assumed to be in the wrong, and it
is up to its driver to establish innocence. When you add to that a corruptible
police system, the matter gets even more complex and unfair. The Caterpillar
driver was very much aware of this warped logic that assumed that vehicles
could only be moving forward during an accident. Moreover, because his
tractor had had no dent, the driver just wanted to make sure he was not liable
for Rich's damaged vehicle. My guess was that he would have to pay for the
expenses himself had he been found at fault. Many employers in East Africa
can summarily dismiss their employees for getting into accidents that incur
the company huge costs in repairs. I was now sure I was going to miss my
flight. I had to get to the airport right away. Yet, I was sad to leave my friend
in this predicament. He said that he anticipated he would need some money
to deal with what was now emerging as a traffic offense. I tried to tell him that
I had to leave, but he was not quite following what I was saying although he
managed to smile. He even managed a wave as I approached a taxicab that
had just pulled into the gas station. I was lucky to get the cab driver to take
me to the airport. I paid him upfront and gave Rich the rest of my Tanzanian
shillings including the earlier-agreed-upon gas money. He was going to need
every penny now. It was a sad departure, but I had to go.

This story speaks of hopelessness and powerlessness and, indeed, symbolically represents the power differential between the powerful (Caterpillar) and the poor and weak (Ford Fiesta). Here is a young man whose lack
of social connections and economic power rendered him almost helpless in
a situation in which he had been wronged. The Caterpillar driver by virtue
of being an employee of a powerful company had some leverage to get out
of an accident even if he was in the wrong. Because the Caterpillar had not
been damaged, and Rich's car was behind it, it seemed almost an act of fate
that the burden would all lie on Rich's shoulders. Had Rich been the son of
a powerful politician or a tycoon or if he himself had been a powerful politician or tycoon, however, the story would have changed quickly as political
clout and money would have changed the power relations attendant in that

scenario. Anthony Appiah shares a similar case of a timber truck backing into and breaking the windscreen of his friend's car in which Appiah was traveling while in Takoradi, Ghana. Similar to my and Rich's ordeal, Appiah's case had many local witnesses, but none was willing to blame the truck driver for the accident. Appiah concludes that the local witnesses were cognizant of the material differences between the two—the car driver (a European) "who could afford to pay for his own windscreen and the truck driver who was an employee who could lose his job and his livelihood" (1993, 8). Why didn't the police immediately side with Rich, who had witnesses willing to validate the fact that the Caterpillar driver was at fault? Why were the police uninterested in the details of the accident and were willing to blame Rich for the accident? Rather than see the legal system as a failed instrument for lack of correspondence with local values (Appiah 1993), I see it as an apparatus that is manipulated by the players based on their actual or relative power to each other. It makes a lot of sense considering how things turned out for Rich and the Caterpillar driver after I left the scene.

When I visited Rich in the summer of 2007 and asked about the accident, he mentioned that things turned out for the better for him despite the initial scare. His friend Saidog, who had been in the car with us during the accident, decided to play "the artiste card" as Rich put it. A Tanzanian of Asian descent had stopped at the gas station to witness what was going on, and Saidog asked him if he could help mediate between the driver of the Caterpillar and the police officers. Saidog mentioned that Rich, even though he was the victim, was reluctant to use what power he had as a musician, because those who knew him might then not think highly of him. The Asian man, I was told, called the police officer to the side and talked with him, or, as Saidog said, "*Akamtetea Rich* (He pleaded on behalf of Rich)." That conversation, as Rich and Saidog told me, changed everything, and Rich was no longer the one in the wrong. The police officer came to him and asked if he was an artiste, and Rich said yes and joked with him, asking if he had not heard his songs. At the end of it all, Rich was not charged with a traffic offense and had the Caterpillar driver promise that his company would assist Rich in getting his car repaired. I could not believe the turn of events. I had all along assumed that Rich was charged and had to pay for repairs for the "Escalade" on his own. As I contemplated this new version of the story, I realized that Rich did have "soft power" as a hip hop artiste, and that this came in handy in times of need.

I remembered Rich narrating a similar scenario when he was arrested for a minor traffic offence. He mentioned that he had been taken to the police station; the officer in charge recognized him as an artiste (*msanii*) and instead of charging him he let him go saying, "*Nenda, nyinyi wasanii mna tabia ya kutuimba* (Go, you artistes have a tendency to castigate us in your songs)." Rich got away with this minor offense because of his position as a public critic of social issues in Tanzania. This role was recognized by the police officer and probably by the Asian man at the gas station in a way that gave Rich leverage in an otherwise imbalanced power relationship. By giving Rich this leverage, hip hop music is therefore realigning some local power relations and reflecting the localization of a genre of music born of contemporary, global cultural flows. The accident scenario also speaks of the broader reality of youth in much of East Africa and their marginal economic and political power and agency. It speaks of a weak nation-state that has been corrupted by scarce resources, which, in turn, creates opportunities for those who have access to and control of the resources to exploit the politically and economically marginalized.

Hip Hop and Social Consciousness in East Africa

As a hip hop musician, Rich has a certain public presence that is not enjoyed by many of his peers. Music is an important platform for social commentary (Askew 2002; Ntarangwi 2003c), and musicians occupy certain important spaces in the communities where public discourse is often dominated by politicians or agents of *maendeleo* (development). Because of its contemporary and unbounded nature, hip hop has come to embody a specific public function—providing a forum for youth, who for a long time have lacked political or economic agency to express and assert their own presence in challenging political, economic, and social processes brought and shaped by contemporary globalization. No doubt youth in East Africa have been adversely affected by the collapse of politicoeconomic structures in the twentieth and twenty-first centuries as orchestrated by, among other factors, colonial legacy, internal mismanagement, and a rigid perception and push for a monolithic notion of development brought by a neoliberal, market-driven economic structure. Yet, it is this same collapse that has forced the youth to creatively confront the collapse's socioeconomic ramifications and build alliances to positively navigate the challenges of SAPs and globalization as shown by scholarly work in other parts of Africa (see, for instance, Chalfin 2000 and Perry 2000, for examples from Ghana and Senegal, respectively).

The economic and political marginalization of youth in East Africa carried over from the era immediately after independence has not deterred them from using survival tactics such as street vending and social networks (see Ogawa 2006), often embracing many facets of different cultural traditions in order to deal with competing realities of being African in a global context that wishes to see the continent as just a "shadow" (Ferguson 2006). To their advantage, the youth have had at least some basic formal schooling that inculcates Western values while also keeping them rooted in their own local cultural traditions in another form of "vernacularization" of dominant cultural ideologies. In this way, they can easily travel through and inhabit different cultural spaces that reproduce in them a certain hybridity that is difficult to tie to a specific locale or ethnicity. This is why hip hop is crucial in the process, as it becomes the epitome of this hybridity in which Western music styles are appropriated into local sensibilities to produce something that reflects the local as well as the global (Magubane 2006; Weiss 2002). Through this music, the youth critique the existing political, cultural, and economic realities and, consequently, join other social and political critics such as the clergy and members of civil society (Haugerud 1995) who have dared to challenge and critique oppressive regimes. Hip hop artistes then become important truth-tellers, especially where some intellectuals, who ought to shape the local critiques of the political terrain, retract when faced with personal and political choices and become "inverted bourgeois" who cannot identify with the plight of the masses (Epprecht 2003).

This role of hip hop artistes is clearly visible to private, social organizations such as Tanzania Media Women Association (TAMWA), which in 2007 commissioned a competition for artistes to compose anticorruption songs in which Mkoloni's song "Tusiogope Kusema (Let's not be afraid to speak out)" took third place.[6] Turning to hip hop as a way of sensitizing the masses of unacceptable public management of resources is important in East Africa where many scholars and critics tend to reject this duty as soon as they get work with the government or when they are seeking favor with international organizations. In Kenya, for instance, many intellectuals and activists who were actively involved in challenging the powers that be in the early 1990s joined the government and turned into their own conservative and combative effigies of what they once fought against. Political critics and intellectuals such as Amos Wako, Kiraitu Murungi, and Martha Karua lost their critical edge when they joined the government or when their friends came to power (Murunga and Nasong'o 2007). Sociologist Chachage Seithy L Chachage argues that in Tanzania, intellectuals at University of Dar es Salaam are complacent and often quiet when it comes to matters of freedom of expression and challenging the Western hegemony that has slowly seeped into the very fabric of intellectual life in Tanzania.[7] Hip hop has become an important alternative to this decline in social critique, and this newly acquired status can be attributed to a number of factors.

Hip hop in East Africa constitutes a new trend in music making and consumption that is unprecedented. Following a wave of multiple commercial radio and television stations that came with economic neoliberalism, as opposed to the state-owned and state-controlled ones of the past, the desire and demand to compete for a customer base to draw lucrative advertisement, forced new radio and television stations to diversify their products (Bourgault 1995). Further, access to recording and studio equipment that came within this time period led to the local production of high-quality music that was available for airplay in the now-growing private radio stations. For a fee, a young and upcoming artiste could walk into a recording studio and come out with a high-quality compact disc of his/her debut single that could be played on one of the newly instituted FM radio stations in his/her respective city or country. Add to this the availability of numerous musical tunes on such computer software as Fruit Loops and the possibility of selling one's music through the Internet, and one has a new space for youth to advance themselves through music and produce high-quality, local music.[8] More recently, many artistes have opened their own recording studios as is the case of Mr. Ebbo of Tanzania, who has Motika Records, Mesach Semakula of Uganda, who has Kann Studios, and Kenya's Ukooflani Mau Mau with Andaki Studios. In this way, they have control over the production of their music while also availing resources to other artistes who may be unable to afford mainstream commercial studios. Andaki Studios, for instance, is available to many members of Ukooflani Mau Mau at lower rates than one would pay at other studios in Kenya.

Theorizing Youth and Hip Hop in East Africa

Research on popular music in East Africa shows that music is an ideal tool through which to assess a variety of cultural realities of a given community or society. Music has been regarded as a way of reasserting an erstwhile African identity (Samper 2004), as a means of negotiating modernity (Nyairo and Ogude 2003; Roberts 1965), and as a reflection of everyday sociocultural youth realities (Lemelle 2006; Ntarangwi 2007; Weiss 2002). Some scholars have specifically looked at how gendered identity is mobilized through popular music (Mwangi 2004; Nannyonga-Tamusuza 2002; Ntarangwi 2003c) while others have explored, in general terms, how national politics and imaginations of statehood are constructed or mobilized through popular music (Askew 2002; Rebensdorf n.d.; Wekesa 2004) and how opposition politics expands through popular music (Haugerud 1995; Katumanga 2007). All these scholars show clearly the value of analyzing music as a window through which to understand local and national social, economic, and political realities by emphasizing music performance as a conversation and a mode of interaction that are fundamentally emergent, undetermined, and contingent. Some marginalized groups use music as a way to exercise power to reconfigure national culture and identity, which are in constant flux (Ferrari 2007; Nyairo and Ogude 2005). Sometimes, it is the language selected by popular musicians that enables them to articulate certain localized identities of ideas appropriated from elsewhere as the youth in Tanzania and Malawi have done (Fenn and Perullo 2000; Perullo 2005). At other times, it is the themes and messages of the songs that shape and define their music (Casco 2006; Perullo 2007).

Many other scholars have shown that hip hop music is very much linked to the politics of identity among youth. Richard Ssewakiryanga (1999) analyzes the emerging youth culture in Uganda where American popular music has become an important framework from which to develop local hip hop culture. He argues that although this music may have important contributions to the local hip hop scene, it becomes localized through a process of reinterpretation and redeployment. Alex Perullo (2005) looks at how rap music confronts stereotypes about young people by using politically and socially relevant lyrics to reach a broader listening audience in Tanzania. Both Aurelia Ferrari's (2007) and David Samper's (2004) work on rap in Kenya show that rather than mere copycats of American hip hop music, the youth invoke traditions of revolution associated with the anticolonial movements such as the Mau Mau to symbolically critique postcolonial realities of cultural colonization.

At times, popular culture, rather than taking cues from the political process, ends up influencing not only political imagination but also its public expression as is the case of the Kenya hip hop duo Gidi Gidi Maji Maji's song "Unbwogable," which was appropriated by the 2002 Kenyan political bloc that ousted President Daniel Moi's twenty-four-year rule (Hofmeyr, Nyairo, and Ogude 2003; Nyairo and Ogude 2005). Looking specifically at reggae musician Bob Marley's legacy, Eileen Moyer (2005) develops an argument that shows how poor and disenfranchised youth in Dar es Salaam mobilize Marley's message of revolution to make sense of their material conditions. Peter Remes's (1998) work in Tanzania shows how language is used to create urban identities among youth while mobilizing certain images of the West, especially, urban Black youth, to curve out a space for expressing an imagined as well as lived reality of urban Tanzania.

Despite this growing research and scholarship on identity and music in general and hip hop in particular, understanding of identity, social critique, and even political consciousness in East Africa as mobilized through music remains limited to conceptual difficulties of localized boundaries that ignore the globalization of music production and consumption that traverse regional territories to disrupt neat national or ethnic boundaries. Many scholars have tended to focus on hip hop within specific countries, ignoring growing cross-border exchanges within East African hip hop, collaborations in recording music and performances, and the emergence of a genre locally referred to as *utake* music (denoting Uganda, Tanzania, Kenya). Tanzania's AY (Ambwene Allen Yessayah), Kenya's Juacali, and Uganda's Babaluku, for instance, collaborated in a song "Utake Anthem" in which they celebrate this regional musical convergence. The value of such collaboration showed when the song won the 2007 Pearl of Africa Music (PAM) award in Kampala, Uganda. In the song, the artistes say,

> More great things are yet to come
> There is no problem we are fine
> We may have challenges but we love each other
> There are no borders, there are no problems

This cross-border and regional reality is stifled by scholars with the analytical tendency to privilege the intersection between politics and geographical location as the trigger for identity formation and analyses.

This current volume methodologically and intellectually transcends such a limiting analysis of the import and outcome of identity and music making to look at how youth mobilize hip hop in order to produce not only new avenues for identity formation but also establish new parameters for critiquing the advent of neoliberal market fundamentalism and share social and cultural interpretations within a broader regional polity. The current volume shows that rather than limiting understanding of youth identity and agency to fixed locales of nation-states, one does get a better picture of the vibrancy of youth engagement with hip hop through a panoramic lens of regionalism and transnationalism aided by global structures of electronic exchange. It is a study based on the flows of music and people beyond their national boundaries, allowing for a perspective on ideological as well as material connections among artistes in Dar es Salaam, Arusha, Nairobi, Mombasa, Kampala, Jinja, Moshi, and Kisumu, to name but a few centers of this music production. I do this without effacing the importance of national political boundaries (as is evident in requirements for passports and claims to social services as citizens of a specific nation) but by showing the constant flow and exchange of music and ideas that would not have been possible in 1989, for instance, when I started doing research on music in Tanzania. Indeed, shared colonial and postcolonial histories as well as attempts to have a unified regional body such as the East African Community (EAC)[9] points to the local awareness and importance of this exchange and flow of goods, ideas, and capital. The messages carried in various hip hop songs across these borders gain transnational appeal and relevance because of this shared history as exemplified by "Utake Anthem." Many are the examples of this kind of cross-border collaboration.

When Maurice Kirya from Uganda and AY from Tanzania collaborated in their song "Binadamu (Human being)," for instance, they were expressing not only a shared sense of musical style but also a philosophy and identity about the plight of young people in Africa that traverses political and cultural boundaries. This explains why they open their song focusing on the troubles that beset poor people: "This is AY from Tanzania, Maurice Kirya from Uganda, a dedication for all Africans living in poverty." To further show their extent of collaboration, they sing in Kiswahili, English, and Luganda (the three main languages of Tanzania, Kenya, and Uganda). There are also numerous other regional music collaborations and exchanges, such as those in which popular Ugandan musician Jose Chameleone's song "Bomboclat" (a Jamaican expression meant to convey shock and awe) borrows its tune from the song "Starehe (Pleasure)" by Tanzania's Ferooz, Prezzo from Kenya collaborated with AY in the song "Nipe Nikupe (Give-and-take)," Misosi from Tanzania and Redsan from Kenya collaborated in the song "Heshima (Respect)," and Uganda's Maurice Kirya, Tanzania's Pauline Zongo, and Kenya's Suzanna Owiyo collaborated in composing and singing "East African Anthem," a medley of the national anthems of Kenya, Tanzania, and Uganda. As Stevens Muendo and Tony Mochama (2007) state, "More artistes from across the border are using the collaboration game as their new strategy to finding acceptance and winning fans across the three countries" and showing the strategic economic choices being made.

This collaboration and border-crossing has confused a number of people wishing to pinpoint the musician's ethnic and national identity. At one time Uganda's Chameleone was thought to be a Kenyan musician, maybe because he jump-started his music career in Nairobi, Kenya. This would explain an incident in which Chameleone, along with Kenya's Redsan, were invited to curtain-raise for Shaggy, a star of raga (hip hop with digitized backing instrumentation) during his Bombastic Kenya Tour in 2002. Some of the organizers had assumed Chameleone was Kenyan and hence the invite. These and many other incidents point to the fluidity of geographic and cultural boundaries when it comes to music performed by East African youth. East African youth have become what Toby Miller (1998) calls "cultural citizens," who, while confined to locality (nation-state) by access to rights and privileges that are availed to citizens, participate in cultural and ideological practices that are beyond the nation-state. Or as Nadine Dolby argues, in her analysis of a Big Brother Africa television show, popular culture "provides a forum that [is] unique in several ways. . . . [I]t [is] watched and engaged by youth; it extends beyond the borders of a particular nation; and it [is] largely beyond the control of the state" (2006, 40).

My argument is that East African hip hop and the processes that lead to its production, consumption, and circulation is for the most part predicated upon a global consciousness that uses expressive culture not only as a politicoeconomic space for youth but also as one that is uncontrollable by the institutions and powers that otherwise structure social discourse and identity within the confines of the nation-state. It is a music form that transcends national as well as regional identities in order to embrace a regional, transnational, and global identity. In this way, hip hop also goes through a process of vernacularization (Appadurai 1996) in which local cultural forms of expression and livelihood, sometimes overwhelmed by a Western hegemony are able to "assimilate and indigenize significant elements of Western culture while still retaining a sense of cultural integrity" (Magubane 2006, 209). By seeing hip hop in East Africa through this transnational paradigm of global flows, I am able to analyze and acknowledge the fluidity of political, cultural, and geographic borders and the resourcefulness of youth even under the most oppressive global conditions.

This project also provides an alternative focus and analysis from that of many scholars of East African music and hip hop who have not placed song lyrics within relevant socioeconomic and political realities. Contextualizing lyrics has enabled this work to show how song lyrics act as metasocial commentaries that are critical in the understanding of transnational interpretations and responses to postcolonial economic and political challenges in East Africa. The current volume studies lyrics that are used as social forms of critique that are locally produced and mobilized to make sense of everyday realities from the perspective of the local while providing an analytical, anthropological distance to make meanings accessible to a wider audience. The focus on lyrics and their contextualized performance allows simultaneous analysis of how hip hop homogenizes youth cultural identity in East Africa by directly appropriating American hip hop to allow for transnational notions of identity while distinctly drawing on its roots as an authentic space for youth contestations of nationalized and even globalized forms of self-actualization and relationships to others. The current volume also shows how the artistes conceptualize the layers and borders of identity that cut across ethnic, national, regional, and global terrains.

The analysis in this work is guided by symbolic-interpretive and comparative approaches to the performance of hip hop, modernity, and identity in East Africa. A symbolic-interpretive approach considers culture as a combination of meaningful symbols and processes to which humans assign meanings in order to understand and deal with social realities (Spencer 1996; Geertz 1973). A comparative approach considers the role played by hip hop and its consumers and producers in different physical locations that embody local and imagined global identities within broader regional and temporal contexts. Hip hop lyrics, musicians' performance contexts, and fan responses to the music are themselves symbols that contain multiple meanings that point to the imagined, represented, and reinterpreted sociocultural realities of youth in different locations in East Africa and beyond (Ntarangwi 2003c).

The research and writing of this book also reflects my ongoing, close association with expressive culture in East Africa as well as my preference for this symbolic-interpretive anthropological approach to culture as performed. In my own anthropological career, I have been drawn to the work of Clifford Geertz and Victor Turner and to those who follow and expand their trajectories as in the case of Sherry Ortner and Edward Bruner. Through their work, I have come to regard culture as the shared ethos and world view of a group or community (Geertz 1973) that is constantly negotiated and reshaped through performance and process (Turner 1974). I find a combination of the theories propounded by these two scholars especially compelling because while Geertz's culture concept is a recipe for the essentialization and reification of groups or communities that could resort in orientalism (Said 1980), it is reinvigorated by Turner's ideas about "social dramas" that provide for social change through "liminality" and "communitas." While attracted to this culture-as-a-system model, I appreciate critiques that have called for new ways that regard culture as practice shaped by power relations, struggles, contradictions, and change (Bruner 2005; Sewell 2005). It is in combining these two views of culture as a system and as practice that I build my analytical frame that agrees with William Sewell and that sees culture as "modified in its effects by the contradictory, contested, and constantly changing ways in which it is implemented in practice while remaining a structure" (Sewell 2005, 88). This culture-in-practice approach fits well with my work on popular culture in which youth, as variably marginalized and dominated subjects and groups, strategically mobilize hip hop as political critique and a tool for cultural survival by essentializing culture. This also follows Ortner to see culture as "embodying some sort of resistance, some sort of mischief, or alternatively as playful and pleasurable, part of making a life on the margins of structures of domination. . . . [Thus] 'culture' . . . is not inherently a conservative or dangerous concept . . . [but] . . . a flexible and powerful concept that can be used in many different ways including, most importantly, as part of a political critique (2005, 36).

The analysis in the current volume shows that the youth sometimes prefer to mobilize an essentialized concept of culture as political critique while they grapple with the issues of cultural and social identity within a world system marked by increased Western cultural hegemony. For such youth, therefore, an essentialized African culture and identity become a powerful tool of resisting being "swallowed" up by the monster of globalization. It is also a tool that allows me as an anthropologist to symbolically access and analyze images, realities, and aspirations of a generation seeking to make sense of a world they seem to have very little control over.

2

Hip Hop and African Identity in Contemporary Globalization

> Mother Africa, you are accused of being the mother of
> HIV, wife beatings, and other problems such as alcohol
> abuse. A black man on TV is so dark it's like he has been
> smeared with GV. What about Europe?
>
> Poxi Presha, "Salsa Afrique"

Hip Hop Music in East Africa:
History, Context, and Practice

By contrasting the representation of Africa with that of Europe in this ex-cerpted song, Kenya's Poxi Presha enters an ongoing debate among scholars and other critics (e.g., Hunter-Gault 2007; Mayer 2002; Mengara 2001; Mu-dimbe 1988; Piertese 2006; Walker and Rasamimanana 1993; and Zeleza 1997) about the construction and representation of Africa. As contemporary glo-balization increases the availability of news and images from faraway places, it also allows many East Africans to not only see how Africa is represented (especially) in the media but also enables them to make representations of Africa that are informed by global and local realities. Many East African hip hop artists use hip hop to represent Africa and an African identity that takes three prongs: an Africa that stands in great contrast with Europe and the West both culturally and politically, an Africa that is vernacular and traditional, and an Africa that is cosmopolitan, holding onto its traditions while embracing transnationalism and transcultural realities. Indeed, hip hop is itself a good example of this reality of multiple identities, borrow-ing its performative structures from Western musical sensibilities and from African cultural forms. It is in looking at the history, context, and practice of hip hop in East Africa that we can have a broader understanding of why it has become such an important space for youth agency. To begin with, hip hop has broadened opportunities for East African youth to collaborate with musicians from different counties and continents. This is why in the song "All Over the World," a group of musicians allied to Ukooflani Mau Mau from Nairobi, Kenya, for instance, present hip hop as a tool for the unification of all youth and socially conscious people in the world especially those facing similar socioeconomic challenges. In the song, they say,

> We're rollin' thick like the Bible quotin' scriptures of survival
> Touchin' masses upon arrival, hip hop is vital
> Represent your sphere, hip hop is global,
> Represent your sphere, hip hop's universal!

This transnational outlook shapes not only the content but also the distribution of the song. This song won Kenya's Kisima Award for best single in 2004 and was widely received as it was played on Channel O (broadcasting from South Africa) and MTV Base (broadcasting from Ghana) and on many radio stations in Europe. The song's album was produced in collaboration with Rha Goddess, an accomplished artist and political/social activist based in New York, and marked a reinvention not only of Kalamashaka (one of the very first hip hop groups in Kenya) but also of how hip hop music was imagined and performed in East Africa.

No other music style has had such a widespread presence and influence on local music in Africa as hip hop has had within a short period of time, and this transnational and cross-border collaboration in "All Over the World" is a good example. That hip hop is global, as Ukooflani sing, is now a truism (Kelley 2006; Mitchell 2002), and yet the most defining attribute of hip hop is its increased localization (Bennett 1999; Condry 2006; Perullo 2007), where it not only represents local realities in local languages but also follows local structures and expectations of social decorum. Tanzania's Dola Soul, who performs with the group Deplowmatz, sees East African hip hop in stark contrast to mainstream hip hop in the United States. In an interview that appears in a 1999 documentary on hip hop in Tanzania titled *Hali halisi* (Reality) by Madunia Foundation, Dola Soul shows the need to avoid profanity and self-aggrandizement: "Hip hop shouldn't be all about 'I shot your mom . . .' People are dying out there in the streets, people are executed in countries. We want to bring out messages in our rap and tell the people what is going on and how we can change the world to make it a better place to live in."[1]

The role of hip hop music in representing this reality of life reflects similar conditions and expectations of hip hop in its nascent stages in the United States. Since its inception in the 1980s in New York, hip hop's identity and authenticity have been linked to poor, urban Black America in the same way "hard core" East African hip hop is linked to youth in East Africa's urban ghettos. These similarities across both sides of the Atlantic Ocean reveal interesting material conditions that create fertile ground for the emergence of hip hop music. In urban America, hip hop emerged in the 1980s when manufacturing jobs that provided gainful employment to urban families, most of them Blacks and recent immigrants, declined and were replaced by service jobs (Kelley 2006). Many social scientists have recorded higher rates of poverty in United States urban spaces in that same period (see, for instance, Bourgois 2002 and Anderson 1990). Many of those manufacturing jobs moved overseas, some to Africa, but they, too, did not improve the lives of many but instead made them even worse (Dimitriadis 1996; Hazzard-Donald 2004; Kelley 2006).

In the late 1980s and early 1990s, hip hop became one medium through which to make sense of and respond to these conditions of extreme poverty and political quagmire. It provided a much-needed voice and public presence to many youth facing unemployment and political powerlessness. From its direct links to rap music in urban Black America to its localized versions, hip hop music traversed the public sphere hitherto occupied by politicians, scholars, and other opinion shapers, generating not only enormous popularity among young people but also stepping into an expanding vacuum of social, political, and economic commentary. Hip hop provided an arena for youth to project and comment on socioeconomic and political challenges. They used it to talk about their challenges and their aspirations for a better life. For a number of them, hip hop provided an avenue to appropriate a Western world they had only seen on television or heard on radio, because they had primarily been socialized to value Western cultural products.

Through a colonial system of education, in both public and private secondary schools (where many East African youth are socialized), for instance, Western cultural ideals became idolized and a foundation for cultural expression into the postcolonial period (Ntarangwi 2003a). Moreover, with agricultural, judicial, and economic systems heavily tied to Western institutions and markets, many East African youth saw and still see their cultural survival pegged to their ability to be as Western as possible. Western education (through private schools or studying abroad) became prized possessions, and the ability to speak English with a British or American accent set apart the local from the cosmopolitan. Included in this cosmopolitanism is a clear taste for Western cultural products such as music, film, and dance. Binyavanga Wainaina poignantly points out this phenomenon of an emerging local identity based on Western ideals: "We all wanted to study in the US. Those of us who felt we were off-centre, who felt we had a social conscience, and some sort of interest in the future of Kenya, were convinced that study in a small White liberal arts college in the US would provide solutions. We would sit high up in the UN someday, in New York, and direct matters to the satisfaction of our continent. . . . [E]verybody would have to study the classical popular hip hop of the 1980s (2003, 2).

The hip hop music of the 1980s that Wainaina mentions was the music of choice for many urban East Africans at the time. Listening to African music was reserved for the "old" and the unsophisticated. African music was only played on special one-hour slots on public radio and in some select social clubs. Most of the time, radio stations played American R&B and European pop music. This made Western music very popular among many young East Africans. In Dar es Salaam, for instance, budding musicians and other expressive culture entrepreneurs composed their own "hip" music by using the beats and styles of those popular foreign songs but inserted their own lyrics in Kiswahili.[2] This way they could have a piece of the West in a linguistic medium of their own. In Uganda, Richard Ssewakiryanga paints a similar picture of a desire to connect with the West especially through music: "My encounter with popular culture came during my adolescence years in the 1980s. At that time we were mostly attracted to American culture. When my friend's uncle returned from the United States with a copy of *Ebony* magazine, we were drawn by the image of a young man wearing an earring. This image fascinated us and we had animated discussions about it. We listened to him religiously and discovered people like Marvin Gaye with his famous song 'Sexual Healing,' Kool and the Gang with 'Get Down on It,' the English group Imagination and their song 'Illusion,' and Michael Jackson (1999, 24). This cultural imagination continues to shape youth identity in East Africa today but in a more complex way. Wainaina's as well as Ssewakiryanga's narratives about their interaction with Western music and its attendant culture resonates with my own experiences in Kenya in the same period. When I attended college in the 1980s, we listened to the same songs Ssewakiryanga cites. We saw African American popular-culture stars as our role models, representing the kind of modernity that our education would provide for us. I was especially awed by my cousins' "cool" hairstyles that were popularized in Kenya by a U.S. break-dance movie (*Electric Boogaloo*) screened in Nairobi in the mid-1980s. We wanted to speak and walk like those movie stars.

These shared experiences show that despite being resident in three different geographic and political locations, we were all being acculturated into a very similar Western cultural ethos.

The sociocultural context within which this cultural expression emerged coincided with high levels of political insecurities and uncertainties that, for instance, rocked Uganda and Kenya in the eighties with civil strife that saw the exit of President Idi Amin in Uganda and an attempted coup that led to diminished civil liberties in Kenya. For some, popular culture became a safe political form of expression and entertainment as numerous musicians were co-opted into the political machinery for praise-singing and propaganda. Later, as hip hop emerged in East Africa to counter this use of music for self-perpetuation by the state, it did so within tough socioeconomic structures. Eventually, certain cultural conditions favored hip hop's emergence and expansion because of the high value for Western cultural products. The two went hand in hand.

The new, liberalized economic climate and stifled government support for the public sector supported by SAPs saw many new businesses strategizing to take advantage of opportunities availed by this change. Everyone and anyone could sell everything and anything in East Africa (Ogawa 2006). Peddlers of cultural products such as music had booming business; pirating of Western music and film became the order of the day. One could walk along the busy streets of Kampala, Dar es Salaam, or Nairobi and buy any music on video or CD for half the cost of an original copy. Street vendors, complete with television sets and CD players, were at hand to test music before one purchased it. Wearing name-brand apparel and painting on public transportation became new crazes in Kenya. Posters and art on public spaces reflected hip hop culture from the United States (Weiss 2002), and, slowly, rap groups started to emerge in the economic capitals of East Africa—Kampala, Dar es Salaam, and Nairobi—as the state's grip on cultural expression relaxed.

The most-recognized debut hip hop artistes in Kenya and Tanzania were Kalamashaka and Kwanza Unit, respectively, who despite their popularity in the 1990s slowly went into oblivion in the 2000s. In Kenya, Hardstone (Harrison Ngunjiri) was the first artiste to record and release a full-length CD—the title song of the album, "Uhiki (Wedding/marriage)", became a hit in East Africa. Kalamashaka charted the way for hip hop in Kenya with their hit single "Tafsiri Hii (Translate this)," which, besides having a good beat, engaged radical social issues such as unemployment, high rates of crime, poor living conditions, and police brutality to which many young urban dwellers (in poor neighborhoods) could relate. The first lines of the song say,

Translate this! Life here in the city is tough
I lament using the mike, translate this!
Even though we are down, we still have hope

These socially conscious lyrics may have endeared their fans but did not augur well with radio DJs who refrained from playing Kalamashaka's songs often deemed politically dangerous, especially songs such as "Ni Wakati (It's time)" that castigate neocolonialism. Despite a new wave of freedom of expression in Kenya at the time, many radio stations were and still are reluctant to play music that criticizes the incumbent government or Western and global powers. Kalamashaka only had about six years of fame in Kenya's hip hop scene and by 2003 had already dwindled into a life of recluse.[3] In Tanzania, Kwanza Unit slowly disintegrated when one of the key members died and the other moved to Canada.[4] A new style of hip hop, locally known as bongo flava, emerged in Tanzania but mostly centered in Dar es Salaam. Meanwhile a number of other hip hop groups had entered the scene in Kenya, and members of Kalamashaka later remerged through Ukooflani Mau Mau and expanded the hip hop realm to other forms of expression such as drama, acrobatics, and drawing.

In Uganda, one of the earliest hip hop groups in Kampala, the Bataka Squad, emerged in the mid-nineties and rapped in Luganda in a style locally called Luga-flow to denote rap lyrics performed in Luganda. The squad was composed of Babaluku (Silas Babaluku Balabyekkubo) and Krazy Native (Alex Kirya). Other Ugandan popular musicians made it outside Uganda in Kenya or in the West especially as migrants in search of better facilities to record their music. Throughout the twentieth century, Kenya had been the hub for music recording in East Africa following a large British-settler population keen on carrying on with the amenities of Britain in the colony. These facilities attracted many regional artistes to Kenya. The Ugandan hip hop sensations Jose Chameleone and Bebe Cool, for instance, rose to the limelight by recording and performing in Kenya. Both of them had moved to Nairobi in search of better opportunities and gained some urban cultural literacy that enabled them to compose songs in Kiswahili and Sheng, a language and style common to many urban Kenyans. Bebe Cool, quoted in a special report published by Kenya's main newspaper, the *Daily Nation*, explains the reason for moving to Nairobi: "I went to Nairobi because I was desperate. People here (in Kampala) never used to believe in us local artistes. First, they thought we were too young. Secondly, they treated career musicians as if they were criminals in Uganda and anyone who went singing was considered a *muyaye* (a vagabond)."[5] These artistes also sung in other local languages that proved to be important in expanding their popularity. Chameleone, for instance, performed some songs in Luganda that did quite well in East Africa, including "Bageya" (a Luganda name). Besides in Kiswahili and Luganda, Chameleone has sung in Kinyarwanda in an attempt to expand his presence in Rwanda and Burundi, where his music has also become popular. He mentions that he first heard his song "Bageya" in a dance club in Kampala, which was played by a disc jockey who had received a copy of the song's album from a friend in Burundi.[6] This localization and regionalism have led to the popularity of this genre of music because it connects not only with local sensibilities but also opens up other opportunities for music making beyond established genres. This popularity and localization of hip hop and its compatibility with local expressive traditions can raise questions of "authenticity."

Hip Hop in East Africa: New Phenomenon or Old Tradition?

Despite the overwhelming evidence that hip hop, as currently expressed in East Africa, has observable African American roots, it also shares some structural and textual styles with other African traditional forms of expressive culture. When we focus on form and style in rap music, for instance, it bears semblance with praise-singing traditions across East Africa, such as those noted for *nyatiti* (eight-string lyre) players among the Luo in Kenya and Uganda (Barz 2001) and *obukano* (bass lyre) players among the Kisii of Kenya (Varnum 1971). Further, although hip hop may be a new phenomenon in East Africa, ethnomusicologists observe that the characteristics of African music in general (see DjeDje 1999) remain rooted in African musical sensibilities, such as the basic structure of call and response, short repeated phrases, and interlocking rhythmic patterns, which constitute much of hip hop in East Africa. This has led some observers to see stronger links between hip hop in the United States and African music. Pangie Anno from Ghana once told a reporter for BBC World Service, "The source of hip hop is an African tradition, an ancient African tradition of freestyling, which is spontaneous poetry to a rhythmic pattern."[7] Local East African musicians also see hip hop primarily as African in both structure and purpose. Yunus Rafiq, a Tanzanian social activist, hip hop advocate, and cofounder of Aang Serian Peace Village in Arusha, Tanzania, shares this sentiment: "Before the days of colonialism, we had youth groups in different villages that would go to sing at different ceremonies. . . . When the colonialists came, they suppressed these institutions, voices. . . . [A]fter colonialism, the people who became government officials were people who were educated in the missionary schools, educated in the colonial way. But when young people started hearing Hip hop, they kind of got their voice that was taken away from them. . . . There is a very strong feeling that Hip hop is an African tool."[8] Whether hip hop is African or not is debatable, but its role in enabling youth agency in East Africa is unprecedented. By building on indigenous structures, hip hop is transforming and revitalizing the lives, perceptions, and cultures of East African youth by creating a new avenue for communication and offering unprecedented tools for education, empowerment, activism, and entertainment. This transformation is also visible in other local music practices. In Uganda, for instance, the traditional musical style consists of praise singing in the style called *kadongo kamu* (Kariuki et al. 2004). *Kadongo kamu* developed throughout the colonial period as a means to revive a crumbling cultural identity that was being assaulted by Western values. This music, however, had to "be defined in a way that would accommodate the new identity which was a hybridization of foreign and Kiganda cultures, especially in urban areas" (Nannyonga-Tamusuza 2002, 137). Many current popular musicians in Uganda, including Geoffrey Lutaaya and Abdul Mulaasi, borrow heavily from this genre. These other forms have, however, remained local and have not been able to crosscut political, geographic, and cultural boundaries as has hip hop.

Uganda's hip hop music continues to find strength in both traditional and transnational styles. A common style is ragamuffin—a kind of reggae that includes digitized backing instrumentation usually behind dub singing, which is similar to rap music in its focus on rhythmic, assonating, and rhyming words—associated with dancehall reggae in Jamaica. By combining the local tradition of rapping associated in praise singing with the dance-oriented Jamaican beats, many Ugandan musicians have bridged an otherwise-polarized music scene that once projected two different music traditions—the local and foreign. Artistes such as Chameleone, Bebe Cool, and Bobi Wine have all successfully used this style. When I attended a public concert at the national Theater in Kampala in June of 2006, emerging hip hop artistes showcased their talents in a talent-search event sponsored by Club lager, one of the leading beers in Uganda. Of the ten performances I watched, seven of them were in the ragamuffin style (commonly referred to as raga), and many of their songs sounded like those performed by Chameleone. Although at this event there were no female hip hop artistes, Uganda has now a growing number of female artistes such as Juliana Kanyomozi, Blu 3, Angela Katatumba, Irene Namatovu, and Chance Nalubega, among others.

Overall, female artistes only constitute, in my estimation, less than 10 percent of hip hop artistes in East Africa. However, lyrics about women are not absent in East African hip hop and have tended to be dominant in many songs by such artistes as Nameless, Deux Vultures, Nonini, Chameleone, Bobi Wine, Bebe Cool, Kunguru and Lenny, T.I.D., Redsan, the late E-Sir, Klear Kut, and Krazy Native. This scenario is not unusual in East African music, where women have had very little participation in music making, be it as band leaders, composers, or performers (Ntarangwi 2003c). In most cases, women perform such supportive roles as backup singers or as dancers and are often chosen first for their ability to draw the male gaze than for their dancing prowess.[9] Hip hop is slowly changing this East African scene, however, as more women are becoming composers and singers. With more opportunities for music making becoming available, more women becoming economically independent, and East African communities becoming more welcoming of women in public spaces, more and more female artistes will enter East Africa's hip hop scene. In Kenya, for instance, Zanaziki, Mercy Myra, Wahu, Tattuu, Nazizi, and Barbara are examples of female hip hop artistes who have cultivated an important presence in an otherwise male-dominated genre. The entry of more female musicians in the hip hop scene could thus be seen as a new phenomenon in the East African popular-music scene. Tanzania has also a number of female artistes, including Lady JayDee (whose song "Siku Hazigandi [Days cannot be frozen]" topped Channel O's charts in the summer of 2007), Sista P, Zay B, and Rah-P.

As cultural, economic, and political territories opened up in East Africa in the early 1990s, cultural forms mediated through hip hop were transported from the United States (through mass media) to East Africa where they were reshaped and localized. At the end of this process are the final products that are distinctly East African, in a way that is both transient and open-ended. The sounds become indigenized to the local musical patterns, and the lyrics are sung in local languages or slang and continually make reference to local personalities, social spaces, conditions, and events. In 2002, for instance, a song titled "Unbwogable" by Kenya's hip hop group Gidi Gidi Maji Maji utilized a musical pattern of a song earlier performed by a U.S. rap group[10] in a way that specifically localized issues to the sociopolitical terrain in Kenya and also in the language of delivery that blended English, Dholuo, and Kiswahili in the lyrics. In the refrain, the group says, "Who can bwogo me? I am unbwogable!" The word *bwogo* in Dholuo (a language of the Luo of East Africa) is equivalent to the English word *intimidate* or *scare*. By Englishizing it through adding *un* and *able,* the word entered into Kenya's public discourse. *Unbwogable* became a catch phrase denoting a state of not being intimidated or threatened. The song was immediately adopted by the unprecedented political alliance of the National Rainbow Coalition (NARC) as the anthem and mantra for removing the incumbent political party, Kenya African National Union (KANU), from power in the 2002 national elections (Nyairo and Ogude 2005).

Other songs become more regional despite being produced in a specific location, as did the song "Ndio Mzee (Yes, sir)" by Professor Jay.[11] The song explores the tendency of politicians to make unattainable promises to the electorate to get their votes. One does not need to be Tanzanian to connect with the message of this song, but to understand the nuances of its expression, some local cultural literacy is necessary. One of the most popular songs in the summer of 2006 during my research was "Swing Swing" by Kenya's group Kleptomaniacs. The song uses a blend of English and Kiswahili in some lyrics:

> Mr. DJ, let's get started
> You don't have to say it, I already know
> I have beautiful women from all ethnic groups.

I heard this song played more than twice within two hours in dance clubs in Kampala, Dar es Salaam, and Nairobi.

The Ugandan hip hop group Klear Kut has also been quite popular in Kenya where, for instance, it has been invited for live performances such as at the Miss Kenya events. Their songs, sung in Kiswahili, English, French, and Luganda, talk about love, social challenges, and the specific musicians in the group. This localization of hip hop songs makes one's understanding of the music and the identity of its producers and consumers all the more complex. While there are clear geographic and political boundaries in East Africa, hip hop seems to be able to transcend them with ease as it references similar sociocultural and historical realities. This regionalism is further enhanced by media outlets such as the East African Television (EATV), based in Dar es Salaam that plays East African hip hop music quite often and is received widely in East Africa, and some video clips of its recording of East African hip hop artistes available on Youtube. Kenya's Radio Citizen also plays East African hip hop for two hours in the afternoon on weekdays, and the DJ takes turns defining some new terms used by musicians, especially those from Tanzania.

Given this emergence of a hip hop culture in East Africa, a number of questions arise. What are the various ways in which hip hop music projects and constructs African identity in this era of contemporary globalization? What images of Africa do youth in East Africa mobilize to define themselves? When pondering these questions during various field research visits in East Africa, I recalled the advice that David Suggs once received from his doctoral advisor about conducting field research: "If you want to know what people do, don't ask them" (2001, 22)—Suggs would be best served observing and participating in many local, everyday activities that, in turn, would generate the right kind of questions and issues to pursue for his research. Although this is valuable advice for any ethnographic research, studying hip hop calls for a different approach, because the songs are already publicly available and often generate different responses and meanings from the consumers. It is these meanings and responses that led me to the music of a number of East African artistes including Kenya's Poxi Presha and Ukooflani Mau Mau, Tanzania's Mr. Ebbo and Professor Jay, and Uganda's Bebe Cool and Chameleone. I had listened to a number of these artistes' songs, followed their careers as reported in the local media, and was interested in their stories. I wanted to meet with them, find out what shapes and motivates their music, especially their lyrics. What was the relationship between their lyrics and their own personal experiences? What were their thoughts on current political culture and their country's sociopolitical history? Who were their role models, and what role did they see themselves playing as artistes in shaping and expressing youth and national culture? How did this relationship inform any of their ideas about identity?

Answers to these questions are addressed in this and other chapters as I analyze different songs by different artistes and tell certain parts of their stories. Yet, of all the issues that emerge in these stories, identity is the most central. Identity formation is fluid and processual, yet many of these artistes attempt to project a concrete and bounded African identity. For the most part, powerful forces such as colonialism, Westernization, and globalization have shaped African identity. We, therefore, have to consider economic and political realities in defining those identities. The desire to define African identity in local terms and the response to contemporary globalization have compelled many of the artistes discussed here to often reify and simplify African identity. As shown below, for artistes such as Kalamashaka, African identity has to be seen in opposition to Europe and Western economic and political hegemony, while for Mr. Ebbo, it is the lack of an African agency in self-definition that leads to careless aping of everything Western. Ukooflani Mau Mau draws its inspiration from artistes such as KRS-One, Arrested Development, and from revolutionary leaders such as Malcolm X and Marcus Garvey, as shown in the descriptive narrative of a visit to their premises in Dandora, Nairobi.

Questions of identity and what inspires song lyrics can also be extended to cover musicians in Uganda and Tanzania. When I spoke with Fred Mariki (Mkoloni) of the group Wagosi wa Kaya in Dar es Salaam in July 2007, he said that many of their songs are reflective of real-life experiences. In the case of their song "Wauguzi (Medical practitioners)," Fred said that he composed the song after he took his younger sibling, who had cut his hand on broken glass, to the hospital. The medical practitioner on duty asked Fred to open the cut so as to see the extent of the damage to the tissue. Fred refused, arguing that he was not going to undertake duties that the medical staff were paid to perform. This and other experiences led him to criticize the behavior of medical practitioners, especially those who go to work drunk and those who expect to be bribed to offer services they are paid to offer in the first place. These personal stories and experiences accumulated through visiting with musicians in their own spaces allowed for a different sense of their music and personality.

On Sunday, June 4, 2006, I had an opportunity to visit with a member of Ukooflani Mau Mau. I arrived at Ambassadeur Hotel in Nairobi, where I was meeting up with Felo (Felix), a former manager of Ukooflani Mau Mau, who had agreed to take me to Dandora, in the eastern part of Nairobi, to meet and interview members of Ukooflani Mau Mau. As I reached into my pocket to retrieve my cell phone and call Felo to let him know I had arrived, I felt a tap on my shoulder and turned to see Felo's smile announcing his own arrival. He wore a loosely fitting, maroon, cotton shirt, khaki pants, and a pair of sneakers. Although many researchers may not pay specific attention to how they project themselves in the field based on how they dress, I was happy to note that Felo's casual wear balanced my own denim jeans and T-shirt. Being the day was a Sunday, many people around us were immaculately dressed in what is locally considered "Sunday best" clothes. We boarded matatu (commuter Omni bus) number 32 for Dandora, and after twenty minutes of driving through various bus stops, picking up and dropping off passengers, we alighted at a bus stop next to a big store called Lesam. We walked to the "project," Ukooflani Mau Mau's compound, a fenced-in establishment with a metal-sheet gate. Inside were four young men just chatting and seated on a long bench. Felo went to say hello to them as I stood at a distance waiting for his cue. He said hello and then proceeded to greet each one of them by making contact with clenched fists.

I looked around the compound and noticed large murals of African American activist Malcolm X, Ethiopian emperor Haile Selassie, Kenyan freedom fighter Dedan Kimathi, Jamaican reggae-star Bob Marley, rappers Tupac Shakur and Notorious BIG, and a DJ spinning discs. At one corner, just next to the entrance into the rooms (which I assumed were bedrooms) were names of Mau Mau generals who had died in the revolution against British colonialism. It became clear that this was a "wall of fame," depicting all the heroes with whom these youth identified. I started making connections between their song lyrics and the artwork that decorated their "project" walls. Even their name, Mau Mau, made much more sense as I realized that it linked them to a specific sense of African identity. Mungai wa Mbugua makes similar observations of Ukooflani's projected identity: "Group members wear 'Mau Mau University' label T-Shirts to indicate their apprehension of the street as a site of legitimate knowledge" (2007, 54).

When Felo asked about the whereabouts of members of the group whom he wanted me to talk to, he was informed that they were not present at the time. Felo decided to go see if Kang'ethe (commonly known as Kah) was at his house, not too far from the "project." We thanked the young men and went out to look for Kah, who is one of the core members of the Ukooflani Mau Mau and had been a member of Kalamashaka. Because Felo knew the area well, I just followed him. After a ten-minute walk, we came upon a small, brick house surrounded by similar houses, some of them still under construction. Felo knocked at the metal gate and then reached in through the gate's small window and opened the gate. A young woman welcomed us into a living room and told us Kah was still asleep. Even though Felo suggested we would wait, our hostess said that she would wake Kah up. After about three minutes, Kah came out to greet us and said that he had just gone to bed because he and a few friends had stayed up talking until about 6:00 A.M. I looked at my watch. It was 10:00 A.M. I felt bad coming in and interrupting Kah's sleep, but he assured us he just needed a few minutes to have his room ready for us to visit with him. He went back to his room, and we were welcomed into his mother's living room where we did not stay long, because a few minutes later, Kah called us into his room.

Kah's "shack" is a single room with a bed, television set, guitar, large speaker, and DVD/MP3 player. I assumed he has his meals at his mother's house as there was no evidence of cooking in his room. Kah has a youthful face and wears long dreadlocks, signaling an interesting connection to Bob Marley and Mau Mau generals, who all wore dreadlocks. Indeed, I would argue that dreadlocks have come to be associated with artistes much more than any other people in Kenya. I sat with Kah for almost two hours talking about music, art, and life in general and was intrigued by his knowledge of world politics and his commitment to African self-determination. Kah oversees the Maono Art School based in Dandora, where youth from the neighborhood are taught acrobatics, drawing, capoeira, painting, and soccer. Kah told me that a team from Maono already was participating in a soccer tournament in the neighborhood. He is well traveled and talked about his time in Holland, Italy, and other parts of the world where he was invited for performances. Showing his grasp of the contexts within which global hip hop occurs, Kah told me, "Corporate America killed hip hop by taking the voice of the youth from the street and turning it into a product." He then went on to tell me that Ukooflani Mau Mau was trying hard to avoid this corporate takeover, despite the many economic challenges they faced as musicians. He said he wanted their songs to remain true to the socioeconomic realities of youth in places similar to Dandora.

As lunch hour approached, I suggested that we go out and sample the local cuisine. Kah said he knew a place where they had already grilled meat, and we all agreed to try it out. On our way, Kah called another member of the group on the phone and asked him to meet us with a few T-shirts they had made so I could purchase some. The lunch place was very busy, and we realized it was a popular spot for locals in search of grilled or boiled meat. We selected the pieces of meat we wanted and found a table. We ordered *ugali* (a popular corn meal that has the same consistency as cake) and spinach to go with the meat. Our conversation was quite a strain as we struggled to keep our voices above the loud sounds of a local comedy in one of the Kenyan languages emanating from the television behind metal grilles on the wall. We talked about the mounds of garbage a few meters away from where we were having lunch and the health hazard they posed for local residents. We turned to politics, and Kah said there was need for local youth to be mobilized to vote for political candidates who would address the needs of the youth directly. Felo mentioned that there was a scheduled political rally later that afternoon at the famous Kamukunji grounds. I asked if we could attend, and Kah mentioned that members of Ukooflani had been invited to perform.

My conversation with Kah made it very clear that he was a very articulate, focused, and well-informed young man and reminded me of U.S. feminist critic bell hooks, who believes that literacy is critical for social change. Indeed, public icons such as Malcolm X were self-educated and developed perspectives and desire for social change through literacy. By literacy, I do not just mean ability to read and write but also—and especially—reading relevant material. It is very easy to assume that youth like Kah are not as "informed" as our more "educated" elites, yet talking with him made me realize that organic intellectuals like him have a lot to contribute to the intellectual discourse of East Africa's public culture. He was conversant with the history of colonialism, the shape of imperialism, and the threat of globalization as an incarnation of colonialism. Much of this knowledge is gained through his own efforts, because with just a high-school education, he would have to glean such history from other sources.

Although Kah did say that "globalization favors developed nations," I could tell that the process of globalization enabled him and his colleagues in Ukooflani Mau Mau to reach many of their fans in East Africa and beyond. He is in close contact with Black scholars and activists in the United States and has received some literature on such issues as the feminization of the Black male from a friend in the United States. These transnational global flows of ideas allow for the sharing and exchange that often constitute the lyrics that Kah and others in Ukooflani come to mobilize in the critique of neoliberal economic structures that favor developed nations in the West. These flows also allow East African artistes to build networks of fans and even consumers of their music. Muki Garang, another Kenyan hip hop artiste, told Reuters's *Africa Journal* in Nairobi that as an underground hip hop artiste, the only way his music can be marketed is through the Internet.[12]

Because Muki's music, like that of Ukooflani Mau Mau, hardly gets airtime on local radio stations due to all the bureaucracies, red-tape processes, and critical lyrics involved, he relies on the Internet for sales and promotion of his music. He also sells his music locally by distributing it personally at "strategic" places such as the monthly hip hop talent show sponsored by the British Council in Nairobi. The questions that emerge from looking at how hip hop is mobilized to respond to various socioeconomic and political realities are: How do the youth perceive themselves? How do they construct who they are in such contexts? Does having access to a world outside their locality through the global flows allow for a specific process of self-identification?

Hip Hop and Youth Identity in East Africa

One of the most visible effects of the current globalization of culture is found in the relationship between youth and their sense of identity. Such identity can be gathered by a quick analysis of language and dress. It is often quite common to see East African hip hop videos where the musicians are in shorts, long white T-shirts, work boots, and baseball hats turned backwards or sideways as one would see on MTV videos featuring U.S. rap artistes. It is also quite common to see artistes in oversize T-shirts embroidered with U.S. professional or college basketball or football teams or players or European soccer-team jerseys. There are artistes who also sing songs that glorify money and bling bling. This media-generated image of hip hop stars is an important trigger to questions of identity and self-representation within larger contexts of global cultural flows.

Kenya's hip hop artiste known as CMB Prezzo (Jackson Makini) has taken this U.S. hip hop artist image to a new height in Kenya. Seeking to reproduce a certain global (stereotypical) image of stardom, CMB Prezzo often defies local logic. He, for instance, created a spectacle in Nairobi in 2005 when he hired a helicopter to drop him at the Carnivore restaurant from Wilson Airport to a *Chaguo la Teeniz* (Choice of the youth) ceremony that celebrates local artistic talent. The spectacle was not only because the trip cost him an equivalent of $1200 but also that the distance covered was less than half a mile. Quite telling also is that CMB stands for Cash Money Brothers, and Prezzo is a local corruption of the word *president,* and, hence, his stage name stands for "Cash Money Brothers' President." It is no wonder that he is locally known as "action Jackson" or "king of bling."

We have to, however, go beyond these physical attributes of identity that can be gathered by what artistes wear and explore how various artistes use their music to bring out multiple notions of African identity. For many of them, being African is partly a product of their cultural imagination as well as lived material conditions. Artistes seeking to express their identity via the lived experiences never quite regard African identity as a fluid and negotiated entity as many scholars would suggest. As Anthony Appiah argued (1993, 286), "[W]e are Africans already [because] . . . being-African already has a certain context and a certain meaning," and Archie Mafeje argues, "African identity is a self-imposing concept . . . [and] Africans know and have always known that they are Africans" (2001, 18). While I am sure many hip hop artistes know that they are African in this "obvious" way stated by these scholars, these artistes also understand that being African means different things to different people. For artistes such as Kalamashaka, African identity is closely tied to socioeconomic issues that pit Africans in unequal relations with Europeans, especially through structures of domination such as colonialism and neocolonialism. They think of African identity as Archie Mafeje does in another context, "as a necessary condition for resisting external domination but also as a necessary condition for instituting social democracy in Africa" (2001, 19). In their song "Ni Wakati," Kalamashaka give an example of this African identity:

It's time for Africa to stand up! it's time for the youth
Open the eyes of your mind and see that what kills you is within you
It's up to you, only a fool forgets his/her history
Thatcher didn't abandon Reagan! Why is it then that Africa
     was abandoned?
I am talking about independence in 1963, the day we were cheated we
     were free
And a philosophy of a hopeless society, Man eat man, man can't plan
Whiteman society IMF and subsidies, and like beggars we continue to
     stretch our hands

Africa's colonial legacy and the new structures of economic domination ushered in especially through measures associated with U.K. and U.S. leadership under Margaret Thatcher and Ronald W. Reagan, respectively, contextualize Kalamashaka's construction of African identity. It is an African identity that is based on race and the structural inequalities that shape the racialized relationship between the "Whiteman's society" and Africa. Political independence did not make African nations completely free, as they continue to be dependent on Western countries for economic and political survival (Isbister 2006; Rodney 1973; Thomas-Slayter 2003). As Kalamashaka's song shows, African nations are still under external domination, and Africans are caught up in an exploitative relationship with the West through institutions such as the International Monetary Fund (IMF) and the Group of Seven, the G7 (now the G8). To be African under such circumstances means to be subordinate to Europe and to live in a society guided by economic structures that cannot completely benefit Africans.

This song is heavily influenced by Malcolm X and the ideology of Black power and racial separation that explain the kind of African identity Kalamashaka presents. In this regard, it is instructive to note that the song's prelude is an excerpt of Malcolm X's speech "Message to the Grassroots,"[13] given on November 10, 1963, in Detroit, Michigan. In that speech, Malcolm X talked about nationalism, using the example of the Mau Mau and their claims to land occupied by White settlers:

There's been a revolution, a black revolution going on in Africa,
     in Kenya
The Mau Mau were revolutionaries
They are the ones who brought the word Uhuru to the fore
The Mau Mau, they were revolutionaries

Kalamashaka now are part of Ukooflani Mau Mau, their music group is collectively referred to as the "Mau Mau camp," and their premises, which I visited in Dandora, have images of Mau Mau generals on the wall. This combination of Malcolm X talking about a revolution led by Mau Mau and a hip hop song by a group who regard themselves as the Mau Mau camp has great symbolic value. Malcolm X is historically known for fighting against White supremacy and calling for racial separatism. He is especially embraced by many Black youth as an icon of Black and African pride in a White-dominated society. Yet, what I see as the most important link among Malcolm X, the Mau Mau, and Kalamashaka is the question of land—its ownership and access. Africa's daunting task in the era of contemporary globalization, as it was during colonialism, remains the question of land. This has recently been demonstrated in two examples—the case of Zimbabwe where White farms were taken over by Black Zimbabweans under the instigation of President Robert Mugabe's government and Kenya's so-called ethnic clashes of 1992 and 1997 and after the 2007 elections, in which many lost their land and lives, especially in Rift Valley province. Land ownership and distribution are such volatile political issues that many politicians, both from the government and opposition, choose to avoid it all together during their political campaigns (Haugerud 1995; Kanyinga 1997).

Historically, the Mau Mau was a nationalist movement in Kenya, fighting to remove British colonial rule in the 1950s, especially in response to their alienation from their land occupied by White settlers. This juxtaposition of two revolutionary icons in a hip hop song places Kalamashaka's notion of Africa identity within structural and material struggles that are historically derived. This juxtaposing offers an interesting critique of the relationship among Africa and Europe and Whites and Blacks in contemporary light of East Africa's struggles with neocolonial economic realities. Malcolm X is also an important symbol here for other political reasons. During the euphoria of multiparty politics in East Africa in the early nineties, Malcolm X became a key icon for Muslim youth in both Kenya and Tanzania who wanted a political future shaped by Islam. It was not uncommon to see the "X" sign painted on public walls in Mombasa and Dar es Salaam. In my view, the youth did not embrace Malcolm X purely for religious reasons but rather as an indication of their search for a practical icon and ideology to be mobilized in their quest to be players in the unfolding political arena, especially given their political and economic marginalization. Further, unlike Appiah's contention that "the colonizers were never fully in control as our elders allowed them to appear"

(1993, 7), Kalamashaka show the negative epistemological and moral effects colonialism had on Africans that led to "mental slavery" even after the colonizers left. They note in "Ni Wakati":

> It is up to you to use your brains
> Tight are the chains with which our brains are bound
> We need to free ourselves from mental slavery
> Then you Africans won't insult yourselves
> Look at that person in the mirror,
> Do you see White or Black?
> It's time, isn't it?

African identity has also been constructed by other East African hip hop artistes in ways that are slightly different from what Kalamashaka does here. This construction includes the representation of Africa in the media and especially in contrast to the West. Poxi Presha constructs African identity by making reference to the negative representation of Africa constructed by the West. He does this especially in his song "Salsa Afrique," a rendition of an old song "Le Boucheron (The jewel)" sung in Lingala in the seventies by Congolese musician Franklin Boukaka. The song, as performed by Poxi Presha, blends some of the original Lingala texts with Swahili and English ones to produce a critique of Africa's image in the West as well as the practices of the postcolonial African state. In the song, Poxi Presha says,

> I don't know if it is jealousy, ignorance, or envy
> But Africa I will defend you till I grow white hair
> I have read about you in newspapers and seen you on TV
> Europe is the one that receives the correct cv

As many scholars and critics have shown (e.g., Hunter-Gault 2007; Mayer 2002; Mengara 2001, among others), Western media has continued to produce many stereotypes of Africa. It is these distorted depictions of Africa that Poxi addresses in this song and sees as poorly and maliciously constructed:

> Mother Africa, you are accused of being the mother of HIV
> Wife beatings and other problems such as alcohol abuse
> A Black man on TV is so dark it's like he has been smeared with GV
> What about Europe?
> Life is about Dot Com and MTV, DVD and heavy technology

With all the numerous examples of corrupt governments and power-hungry leaders in Africa, it is often quite suspect to start faulting outsiders for

Africa's political and economic woes (Prah 2002). However, as Poxi Presha shows in this song, Africa's image is also carefully constructed to evoke specific and often negative perceptions, relations, and views. On the contrary, Europe and the West are positively depicted in a way that can lead a casual observer to think that nothing good comes out of Africa and that nothing bad comes out of Europe. What Poxi seeks is a more balanced representation of not only Africa but also other parts of the world, including Europe. He is also very critical of socioeconomic inequities within Africa and especially in Kenya as evident in his rendition of Gabriel Omolo's 1972 hit song "Lunch Time" (see Nyairo and Ogude 2003 for a discussion of this and other of Presha's songs). Poxi Presha died in 2005 fighting for the rights of local musicians who he understood were being exploited and not receiving appropriate payments from producers and consumers of their music.

As global cultural flows expand access to images and products from different parts of the world, local perceptions and constructions of self take on cosmopolitan, fluid, and even essentialized forms. While the last two examples from Kenya provide a construction of African identity that is best understood through race and in opposition to Europe, other artistes give Africans more agency in shaping their identity and often challenging them to be reflexive and self-critical. Mr. Ebbo from Tanzania ties African identity to a sense of personal pride and faults Africans for the negative images they receive, arguing that it is their lack of cultural pride that bedevils them. He brings out this argument in his song "Fahari Yako (Your pride)"

> If you are an African, what is your pride? Or are you a black European?
> If you are patriotic, what is your pride? Don't disregard your home
> Without your roots, what is your pride? Even if [your home] is in a hole
> Without a culture, what is your pride?

For Mr. Ebbo, to be African requires a very deliberate sense of pride in self, pride in who one is and especially in one's African identity. Such pride translates into patriotism and a love for one's cultural roots irrespective of the shape such a stand takes. To lack such pride is to be without a culture. It is interesting that Mr. Ebbo has himself adopted a Maasai cultural identity in his musical performance—wearing traditional Maasai dress and singing in Kiswahili laced with a Maasai accent—even though he is not ethnically Maasai. His hit single "Mi Mmasai (I am Maasai)" publicly constructed this Maasai stage identity that has come to define his artistic life. Being Maasai in East Africa has become the quintessential traditional African identity, and Mr. Ebbo's choice of an icon for traditional African culture could not have been better. In making this choice, however, he falls into the same discourse that was carried over from colonialism to contemporary East Africa in which the Maasai represent noble savages who simultaneously stand for traditional African cultural pride and the antithesis of modernity. The group Xplastaz from Arusha, Tanzania, also refers to their music as "Maasai Hip Hop" even though only one member of their group is Maasai and only plays a very small role in the composition and production of their music.

Placing emphasis on cultural traditions within hip hop helps us understand its role as a platform to discuss and construct African identity. It is also a tool for youth to access an international market for their music by reverting to essentialized "African culture" that affirms the stereotypical image of Africa as backward and unchanging. Interestingly, when these artistes project this bounded and often commodified African identity, they end up showing not only the contested nature of identity but also its performative and fluid nature. Identity only takes concrete form when it is mobilized through performance. Mr. Ebbo expresses this aspect of African identity by faulting Africans for not holding up to the kind of Africanity necessary for creating international presence and recognition, as in "Fahari Yako":

> Many days are gone by and we are not yet recognized
> We are not even heard internationally; what makes our people
>   not to be heard?
> Is it the colonialists who deny us our rights?
> It is our practice of aping aimlessly until we lose direction
> Are other people's cultural products superior to ours?
> If you think it through, you will realize we bring ourselves down

Many scholars have shown the devastating effects of colonialism on Africa's political, economic, and cultural structures (see, for instance, Ake 1982; Comaroff and Comaroff 1991; Pels 1997; Prah 2002, among many others). While recognizing this reality, Mr. Ebbo, however, calls for some accountability and reflexivity on the part of Africans. What role have Africans played in reproducing and perpetuating structures of inequality and cultural erosion? To this end, he thinks that the blame lies squarely with Africans as well, because they have "aimlessly aped" the cultural practices of the West. East African cultural critics such as Ngugi wa Thiong'o (1986) and Okot P'Bitek (1984) have also written against this uncritical consumption and aping of Western cultural practices. Indeed, P'Bitek provides a classic example of an alienated African who after aping Western cultural traditions turns around and loathes anything African. In "Song of Lawino," P'Bitek presents Lawino's husband asking, "What is Africa to me" Blackness, Deep, deep fathomless, Darkness (1984, 125) and then goes on to ask, "Mother, mother, why was I born Black?" (1984, 126). Mr. Ebbo provides specific cultural practices that show this cultural aping and self-loathing:

Start with clothing as well as expressive culture
When you wear like an American, you think you are too hot
While batiks and "vitenge" get faded in shops
"I love New York" and you have never been there
It is not love but confusion

Scholars exploring the place of Western clothes in Africa argue that secondhand clothes have established a clothing culture that has led to the dwindling of the local textile industry (Hansen 2000; Rivoli 2005). In some cases, used clothes have created a substantial industry in and of themselves. Pietra Rivoli (2005) states that America's largest export to Tanzania is used clothing, hence explaining the "I Love New York" clothes that Mr. Ebbo refers to in this song. Mr. Ebbo's construction of African identity aligns well with the socioeconomic realities that are shaped by structural changes that led to the collapse of local clothing industries. Further, many textile industries have been closed down in East Africa not only because of the influx of cheap Western clothes but also because many East Africans prefer to wear imported clothes even if they are secondhand. Through various forms of socialization and enculturation in Western cultural values, many East Africans prefer Western clothing and despise local batiks and "vitenge" (multicolored fabric made locally and used for both male and female clothes). Mr. Ebbo sees such clothing preference representing a condition of self-loathing that also hinges on mental slavery mentioned above by Kalamashaka:

Slave mentality controls you, leading you to wear clothes with
    foreign flags
A Tanzanian named Nyanguleni thinks he is hot bouncing on the road
When foreigners see you wearing those clothes, they laugh at
    you secretly
When you do so, you belittle yourself. If you cannot respect yourself,
    who will?

The message in this song brings to mind a case I witnessed in northern Tanzania in 2001 when I took American undergraduate students on a study-abroad program to an animal-husbandry training institute. The local students at the institute interacted with the American students for about six hours, each group interested in the other's culture and educational experiences. In one question-and-answer session, a Tanzanian student asked the American students what he could do to relocate to the United States. When he was told that America is not as it is depicted in movies, he said that he would rather be in an American jail than live in Tanzania. The American students were shocked at this response and wondered why the Tanzanian student would loathe his own country so much that he would prefer an American jail. The American students suffered the embarrassment identified by James Ferguson when they encountered an African ostensibly begging for "salvation from Africa's problems" (Ferguson 2006, 156). Such cross-cultural encounters may reveal a lot about perceptions of other cultures and countries but more so about some Africans that Mr. Ebbo regards as "mental slaves."

How then do we account for these different ways in which hip hop artistes present African identity? The answer lies in the various ways the artistes and their music encounter and interact with contemporary globalization and the effects it has on the musicians' sense of self, their lived experiences, and their projected image of how life ought to be. The increased presence of goods, styles, and other cultural products from external locations has sometimes produced feelings of invasion and lack of uniqueness. Cheap, counterfeit goods in local markets increase access to electronic and recording facilities, while continued virtual or actual cross-cultural encounters have produced competing realities of artistes' lives and contexts of producing music and identities. This mixed bag of "goodies" brought by contemporary globaliza-tion informs the very process of constructing African identity in which these artistes are engaged. On the one hand, it has availed a space and material for youth to construct various forms of identity while allowing them a platform to critique local political and social realities. On the other hand, this same process of global flows continues to threaten to homogenize economic and even cultural realities in the world and probably erase erstwhile cultural boundaries. In response, some of the youth seek unique self-representation, however distorted or constructed a shape it may take, as others critique what they see as the "contamination" of African culture.

Some artistes have a desire to project a Western modernity through their music, but there is now a greater majority of localized versions of hip hop as well as those that clearly seek to establish themselves as authentically African. Moreover, radio DJs are now quite comfortable playing local music sung in Kiswahili as well as in local urban slang that constitutes a mix of Swahili, English, Luganda, and other local languages, unlike in the past when such music would only be played in specific programs dedicated to local music.

This change in the music scene in East Africa to allow for local songs to be played in mainstream radio stations and clubs ties very closely to the notion of identity addressed in this chapter. An African identity is not only mobilized through dress, language, or other material things. It is also mobilized through values and attitudes towards those material things. To develop and to celebrate a liking for African music in East Africa where there is a high presence of what Appiah (1993) calls "europhones" are no mean feats. Some artistes are changing their music to localize it in different ways. Uganda's all-female band Blu 3, which started their music career singing exclusively in English, for instance, increased their local and regional popularity when they started singing in Kiswahili[14] and later in Luganda. By embracing a local language, they entered into a local moral and cognitive conception that marks the importance of an African modernity. Blu 3's entry into hip hop scene is also an important phenomenon in East African popular music where there has been a marked gender imbalance. Hip hop is slowly but consistently challenging this reality.

3

Move Over, Boys, the Girls Are Here

Hip Hop and Gendered Identities

Women stop sleeping, we must always be strong
Women stop sleeping, let's work hard and move forward
—Zay B, "Akina Mama (Women)"

Performing Gender, Performing Hip Hop

Summer 2005 was an interesting time to be conducting research on hip hop music in Kenya. Besides the period being exactly ten years since the debut of hip hop in Kenya, a lot of new songs had been released into the market as new FM radio stations continued to be important outlets for such music. Moreover, numerous live shows presented Kenya's emerging hip hop music to the now-growing fan base. Slowly, many restaurants around the city were showing preference for live-music performances instead of the usual recorded music that had dominated their entertainment repertoire for years. It so happened that as I was wondering where to go to listen to live hip hop music, a friend of mine, who knew that I was conducting research on hip hop mentioned that there was an ongoing Kenyan music competition at the Klub House in Nairobi's Parklands area. This club is locally referred to as K1 because there is a sister club, off Uhuru Highway close to the industrial area in Nairobi, that is called K2. Both venues are popular with music lovers and attract a large group of youth. My friend mentioned that there was a performance on the coming Saturday if I was interested. I told him I was and noted the date on my calendar. When the Saturday came, I made sure I carried my fieldwork companions—pocket-size notebook and a pen—before leaving for K1.

Many clubs in Nairobi often do not get full until after midnight, so I decided to wait until about 11:00 P.M. before I started my trip to K1. At about 11:20 P.M., I asked the front-desk attendant at the hotel I was staying in to call for a taxi to take me to K1. When the cab arrived, I met with the driver and negotiated for the cost of the trip. We settled on a cost that I considered fair, and we were soon on our way to K1. It took the taxi only fifteen minutes to cover a distance that usually takes an hour or more during rush hour in Nairobi.

We approached the dimly lit entrance to K1. Ahead, I could see a long bar and an equally large restaurant where one can get Kenya's national delicacy, *nyama choma* (grilled meat) accompanied by *ugali,* greens (usually kale and spinach) or *kachumbari* (a mix of fresh onions, tomatoes, parsley, and hot peppers), and other local delicacies. This combination of a bar, restaurant, and dance club makes K1 quite a popular spot in Nairobi and was made apparent from the number of vehicles parked at the premises. There was not a place to park in the enclosed area of the club premises. On realizing that the taxi I was in was making a "drop off," the guard at the gate let the driver go close to the restaurant entrance, from where I alighted.

Many young people were walking in as well as a number of others who just sat in the wooden-wall restaurant talking with mouthfuls of *nyama choma* and warm beer. Watching them reminded me of my undergraduate days in the eighties when music and beer defined our ultimate idea of fun. Now, almost twenty years later, I was not sure I belonged in the Klub House. I consoled myself by seeing it as strictly "business," doing what defines ethnography—participant observation. I knew, however, that the "participant" aspect was limited to just listening to and watching the musicians perform their music. I would do more observing than participating. I chose a quiet corner away from the dance floor but strategic enough to allow me a clear view of musicians on stage and their fans on the dance floor as well as around the stage. I was also comfortable enough to jot down some observations in my notebook. I quickly realized that the large crowd that had gathered in this section of the club came to witness the finals of Kenya's Music Competition. The overall winner, I learned, was to receive the equivalent of a thousand U.S. dollars, a recording contract, and a seven-day fully paid vacation in Egypt. That may explain why the parking lot was full.

I settled into my observational spot just as one contestant was vying for the grand prize. It was a woman named Angela, who sung a Luo song in some American melody that made it sound bad. The crowd was booing her as she tried to tell them, "Wait a minute, give me time," as if to convince them that she was better than she was sounding. In my opinion, she was trying to emulate the famous Luo singer Suzanna Owiyo, who has perfected the blend of Luo lyrics and melodies with R&B tunes. This attempt by Angela had failed completely. Owiyo's songs in her album *Mama Africa* continue to dominate the local and regional music scene. Because I had come to watch some of the popular hip hop artistes whose music I was interested in studying, I decided to ignore this particular performance. After Angela's performance, the master of ceremonies asked the crowd for an applause, but instead they booed. He then quickly announced, "Wahu in the house," to which I got quite excited because I wanted to see how Wahu—now a formidable hip hop singer in her own right—would relate with this seemingly hostile crowd. I had listened to and transcribed some of her music, and Felo, who had once managed Ukooflani Mau Mau, had told me about a duel between her and Deux Vultures, who had sung a song "Kinyaunyau," about a woman who was a "gold digger." Wahu, Felo told me, had responded with her own song "Kibow Wow," in which she stated that the man was an "imitator" and "pretender." Little did I know that she would be performing at K1 and that she would sing that song. Before Wahu came on stage, the DJ played about three songs, all by local artistes.

Back in my day, when Ainsworth on Museum Road in Nairobi was the hottest discotheque in Nairobi, we only listened to European and American pop music. Local music was reserved for an hour or two on Voice of Kenya (VoK), a government-sponsored radio station, while the rest of the time, DJs played foreign music. In the first five years of the twenty-first century, however, local music has dominated discotheques and radio stations. By 2005, over a dozen private FM stations were on the air in Nairobi, and many of them played local hip hop music regularly. Everywhere I had been in East Africa between 1999 and 2005 I realized that local music, especially hip hop, was the music of choice. Indeed, in the three hours I stayed at K1 that Saturday night, I only heard music by East African artistes with Kenyan musicians dominating.

I turned towards the stage as the crowd started cheering, and only then did I realize Wahu had already climbed on stage and was holding a wireless mike. She started walking across the stage asking the crowd to "make some noise." Some people in the audience were jeering, but the majority cheered her on. The cheering increased when she started singing a few lines from her hit song "Sitishiki (I am unshakable)." Dressed in a tight pair of denim jeans and a shiny light-blue blouse that was provocatively cut to show her cleavage, Wahu asked the DJ to increase the volume on the track that was now picking up momentum. As the music got louder, she walked around the stage waving to the crowd and then sang, "*Sitishiki . . . wala sizubai na hizo hela zako ooh* (I am unshakable, neither am I mesmerized by your wealth)" as the crowd (mostly women) sang along and finished the verse, "*Hazinitishi!* (Doesn't impress me)," "C'mon, c'mon, DJ, give me more volume!" Wahu said as she got excited now that the crowd was getting into the performance. As the volume increased, she went on to demonstrate her mastery at reading live audiences and sang relevant songs and specific parts of them. "This man thinks he is a Casanova, this man thinks he is an operator," she sang, and she shoved the mike toward the crowd that was now singing along with her. She stopped singing abruptly and told the crowd, "*Kama hutishiki* (If you are not easily shaken), sing with me!" to which the crowd screamed and waved their arms in the air.

When she resumed singing the song, the crowd was all now singing with her. Her request had worked. This was a song that the crowd seemed to love, and Wahu took advantage of that to make it even more relevant. She threw in a punchy line from the song: "*Maringo yako yaboesha* (Your pride bores me)," casting a glance at a group of men seated at a corner sipping beer and chatting. She went on singing, "Showing off his expensive car, showing off his expensive house," as the crowd now took over and sang louder than before. Then came the part that everyone seemed to have been waiting for: "*Kosa lako ni moja, wafikiri wanitisha!* (You made one major mistake, thought you could shake me)." Someone in the crowd shouted, "*Huwezi!* (You cannot)," and Wahu responded with a thumbs-up gesture.

Wahu seemed quite comfortable in this context and her performance convinced me that I was watching a master entertainer at work. She knew her crowd and she worked them up pretty well. This was quite evident as she sung part of the song laughing, maybe at the man's misguided assumption: "So you buy me a drink or two and expect me to go home with you!" A woman in the crowd said, "Imagine!" The audience was clearly getting into the song and engaging with the realities of the meanings carried in the lyrics. This was exactly what I always wanted to witness; the direct engagement with lyrics and the process of meaning making. Now I could at least see why the song was so popular; a lot of people, mostly women, could relate to it.

As this one faded away, her latest song "Kibow Wow," the response to Deux Vultures's song "Kinyau Nyau," was ushered in as the DJ also seemed to be reading the mood of the crowd and their fascination with Wahu's songs. With the song playing in the background, Wahu moved to the edge of the stage and closer to the fans that were gathered around it and asked them, "Where are the *kibow wow?*" The men booed, but the women cheered. Wahu started the song as a conversation: "*Ati* hook me up with a G my guy (Give me a thousand shillings, my friend)," "*niburudishe kadame my guy* (to entertain my girlfriend, my friend)." She stopped as the song was gaining momentum and asked the DJ to "stop the track." "My girls, I can't hear you!" she shouted, and the crowd screamed back, and then she resumed talking like the character she was criticizing: "*Kila siku* (Everyday), hook me up, hook me up, ha! *Kwani ni nini?* (What is it?)" Then she started singing along with the song that was now being played loud,

> *Ukiniita Kinyau Nyau* (You call me Kinyau Nyau) and then ask for my
>   phone number
> *Na accent moja kali sana* (With a fake accent)
> *Na ndege hajuwahi panda* (And you have never been in an airplane)
> *Hata ile ya Mombasa* (Not even the one to Mombasa)

"You are a liar, imitator!" She then walked across the stage and stopped: "K1, let me see your hands up! Come on, all my girls, sing with me!" and the women joined her in the refrain, "*Kibow wow, soto soto, anapenda nini, joto joto, atoke aende, peleka maringo kule* (What does he like, hot hot, get out, and take your pride elsewhere)" then someone in the crowd shouted, "We love you, Wahu!" to which Wahu responded, "I love you, too!"

This went on for a few more minutes until the song ended. Some cheered while others jeered as Wahu left the stage. The master of ceremonies took the stage and said, "Ladies, let me hear you scream!" and the women screamed as some men booed. Then he said, "Okay, gentlemen, especially if you appreciate some beautiful ladies, make some noise!" Some men cheered and screamed. At this point, I realized that something amiss had just happened. Do men in such a context only cheer a woman because of her physical beauty? Is that what it takes to neutralize Wahu's hard-hitting lyrics that may have made those men boo and jeer in the first place? Is reference to beauty all it takes for some men to stop jeering and scream in affirmation? Did they miss the whole point of Wahu's lyrics? Maybe the master of ceremonies wanted to have a good ending because the performance had gone well, and Wahu had managed to rally support from the audience. She had excited many, especially with her critique of men who tend to use wealth to dominate or intimidate women. This seemed to go well with the women in the audience and not so well with some of the men. To me, this was a display of what happens when roles are reversed, and the dominant group's ideology and practice are placed on a pedestal of critique.

Wahu was representing a new breed of female hip hop artistes who were challenging the common practice preferred by many male artistes to not only vilify women but also commodify them through music performance.

She was inserting a new kind of meaning and thinking into hip hop as it relates to gendered behavior. As a genre that has been historically dominated by men, hip hop was now slowly being appropriated by women. At this live performance, Wahu was able to make specific connections with her fans based on the relevance of her lyrics. In performance, she found avenues of reconfiguring gender ideologies and practice, providing a countercritique of a genre that had thus far been dominated by men and by stories told by men about the world as seen by men. It was time for the men to move over and let Wahu take center stage.

This performance by Wahu was not just a performance that was different and entertaining. It was a performance accompanied by critique and the reordering of perceptions and ideologies about gender. It was a performance by a university graduate who exemplified a breed of young women ready to engage with received norms about women and gender and in effect question their viability and utility. Placing hip hop alongside gender and identity, especially in the context of the above performance by Wahu, reveals gender as a performed entity. Gender gains meaning through performance, through individuals acting in specific ways that can be identified as gendered. Gender is here regarded in the same way Judith Butler does, not as a fixed reality of who one always is but rather what one does (performs) at a particular time. Butler notes that "there is no gender identity behind the expressions of gender; . . . identity is performatively constituted by the very 'expressions' that are said to be its results" (1990, 25). If the woman accepts to go home with a man after he buys her two drinks, as Wahu projects, she is ratifying the expected gender norm of being economically dependent and thus sexually available to any man who can provide such material goods. As in the example of a song by Lady JayDee below, buying or accepting beer carries gendered connotations that define expected masculine or feminine qualities. One cannot ignore, however, that such a choice is also based on one's socioeconomic power.

Hip hop expresses, therefore, the fluidity and performative nature of gender, revealing how normalized gender identities can be reconstituted to gain new meanings. In the same vein, however, we have to note that hip hop also reifies and straitjackets gender in a way that is both liberating and controlling. There are hip hop artists who mobilize and celebrate a critical and interrogative stance on gender, while there are others keen on maintaining traditional and conservative notions of gender. Many of the hip hop artists in East Africa are male because music making happens in public space, and public space has, in most instances, been sanctioned as male space, especially in urban centers where East African hip hop thrives. Wahu's entry into this space seems to disrupt the existing male hegemony that defines what role women can play in public discourse on gender. Booing by male members of the audience at Wahu's performance in K1 can be read as an indication of men's discomfort with Wahu's disruption of expected gender norms. When the master of ceremonies asked for their support based on Wahu's physical beauty, the men cheered in a manner that signaled their desire to restore their dominant position in the existing gender hierarchy through rewarding physical attributes that have often been used to define women's legitimacy for making claims to public spaces. Yet, the core of Wahu's performance was to challenge such gender normalcy. As a result, she was doing in hip hop what Adrienne Rich did in writing poetry, singing "with the haunting sense of being overheard by men, and certainly with the inescapable knowledge of having already been defined in men's words" (quoted in Behar and Gordon 1995, 6). By calling on her female fans to sing along with her when she castigated men who seek to "shake" women while in reality such men are "liars and imitators," Wahu was seeking to revise the social script in order to decenter men as the narrators of the gendered world and insert women as both knowers and articulators of the material that define such a terrain.

Dominant assumptions about women and men that find their way into hip hop songs tend to both reflect and obfuscate the diverse ways that ideas about masculinity and femininity are constructed, imagined, and used in everyday life. Rather than present clear-cut caricatures of gender, they present a multilayered and multifaceted picture of gender as practice and ideology. It is this multifaceted nature of gender, its production, and its consumption that informs my analysis of hip hop music. The songs present examples of men and women who fit the expected social roles and norms, as well as men and women who do not fit those social roles and norms but straddle both paths and the in-betweens. All this has to be understood within a larger sociocultural context. Popular music in East Africa has long been produced and defined by men through a male gaze that narrates male experiences of the world. As a result, women have only featured as additions to an already existing male script or as color to adorn the male canvas of culture. As shown elsewhere (Ntarangwi 2003c), this is only the reality that one finds if one seeks just the idealized notions of gendered behavior in East Africa's music terrain. Granted there are more male hip hop artistes than there are female artistes, and there are more song texts that focus on descriptions or desires of/for women, but such a reality only becomes central if it is assumed that gender issues that favor women are only expressed by women. The reality, at least as shown in my research, is that such an assumption is misleading as there are men who sing songs whose themes favor women and vice versa.

In highlighting this aspect of the artistes and their songs, I am deliberately presenting an analysis of gender and hip hop that has been lacking in much of the now-emerging literature on hip hop in East Africa, which seems to be more focused on nationalism and cultural appropriation.[1] To do a gendered analysis of hip hop music in East Africa succeeds in achieving two things: first, it allows me to reveal the dialectical pattern of subversion and adherence to received sociocultural norms about men and women as will be shown in the hip hop songs discussed in this chapter and, second, it characterizes gender relations within the most commonly acknowledged social relations of motherhood and heteronormalcy. Unlike in the West where we increasingly see challenges to gender norms through the introduction of the "third sex" of lesbian, gay, transgender, and intersex individuals and even the rejection of marriage and motherhood as critical in definitions of femininity, gender identity in much of East Africa is still very much a heterosexual and maternal/paternal-oriented phenomenon. What these hip hop artistes do is try to reorder the existing gender normative values without changing the existing structures that define them all together. To better understand women's and men's perceptions and performances of gender through hip hop, we take into account not their ability to transcend normative gender markers but the meanings that are attributed to those genders. As a result we look at the complexity of people's identities not just gender alone, but its interplay with and enactment in combination with personal histories, economic opportunities, and cultural factors that play out differently in individual's lives. When a man is unable to provide for his family materially, he fails to perform the expected role of a man in the community and thus becomes like a woman, who herself is expected to seek and receive economic support from a man. Such a man becomes feminized because his gendered identity is not easily transmutable from its biological maleness. If he is able to provide economically he can regain his masculine identity that then becomes defined with economic achievement. In this regard, therefore, despite close contact with and influence by Western cultures, youth in East Africa regard and present gender in ways that are clearly defined by the local cultural exigencies and sensibilities.

Hip Hop, Gender, and Local Sensibilities

As the landscape of politics and economics continues to change to include individuals from different social, ethnic, and age backgrounds, hip hop will continue to play an important role in contemporary lives of East Africans while responding to the specific experiences and expressions of gendered ideologies and practices. For one, we can see that hip hop is giving women a better chance to express themselves publicly even though they are usually outnumbered by men. It is also allowing for an interesting gender balance as many men and women pursue this mode of expression, making hip hop a useful medium for mobilizing youth culturally and socially.

Hip hop is not only opening up spaces to discuss gender issues but is also availing a platform for a discourse on other social and cultural issues within a communicative medium that the youth can relate to and control. However, getting this platform is only one part of the challenge because achieving more equitable distribution of contributors to those discourses will continue to be reflective of the prevailing social structure and organization. Consequently, despite that there has been a steady increase in the number of female artistes performing in hip hop since the 1990s when it started taking root in East Africa, when it comes to social commentary, very few female artistes stand out (Mwangi 2004). Indeed, in my own assessment, only Wahu from Kenya and Zay B from Tanzania have consistently composed and performed songs that have texts that challenge the predominant male view of gendered relations. Both these artistes not only challenge a particular male view and construction of femininity but also admonish their fellow women and advice them to cultivate self-drive and belief in their abilities so that they do not have to constantly depend on men. They do this by composing songs that are relevant for all contexts in East Africa and beyond.

The expansive and accommodative creativity that has accompanied African music for centuries is now reflected in hip hop from across different geographical locations. Wahu's song "Kibow Wow" is a response to this expansive and accommodative moment, inserting an alternative (female) voice to the life of partying and of seeing women simply as "gold diggers." At least, the latter is the message that seems to be mobilized in the song "Kinyau Nyau" by the group Deux Vultures, which Wahu is responding to in her song. In the song, Deux Vultures state,

> Kinyau Nyau says she wants a car, a storey house at the coast
> Okay here is the money no problem
> I am a lion, I know what I am hunting for
> Patience pays, just wait till nightfall

Deux Vultures are insinuating that the woman, who is the subject of their song, is only after the man's material wealth and that the reason the man agrees to succumb to her pressure is because he is "a lion on a hunt." They present the woman as unable to fend for herself and, yet, is so demanding of her man. They also show that the man is willing to put up with such pressure simply to get her at nightfall. The symbolism of the lion and nightfall is not lost to those who know the behavior of the king of the jungle—that the king tends to be active at night and uses tactics of ambush and waylaying its prey because it does not have stamina for long chases like the cheetah does. The symbolism is also used to denote notions of masculinity associated with power, physical strength, and being the leader of a group of lionesses and their cubs.

In responding to this song, Wahu not only uses the same melody and beat used by Deux Vultures but also deconstructs the presentation of the man as the provider. She says that the man is not only pretentious but also begs unashamedly. In "Kibow Wow," she says that the man owns none of the material wealth he lays claims to when projecting his masculine identity but has rather borrowed everything from his friend. This "borrowed" image of wealth is what he uses to impress his targeted female "prey." Wahu presents this man's encounter with his friend:

> Give me a thousand shillings, so that I can entertain my girlfriend
> Give me your jewelry, my friend, so that I can show off a little
> Give me your car, my friend, so that I can take her to the club

This man has no money of his own, and yet he wants to project an image of wealth in order to meet the expected or prevailing standards of dating rituals in this context. Wahu constructs the man not as he presents himself in public but as a poor fellow with nothing to his name including the house to which he wishes to take his girlfriend. When he fronts himself as a wealthy man in public, he masks his dependence on other people, including his parents, for everything. This is revealed as Wahu continues to sing:

> You call me Kinyau Nyau, and at thirty years old
> You are still living with your mother and asking your father for money
> Then ask for my phone number, with a fake accent
> And you have never been in an airplane
> Not even the one to Mombasa

The last four lines present another interesting phenomenon that we can connect to colonialism and the cultural imperialism of globalization. As mentioned in chapter 2, many young East Africans want to sound American (for the most part), and this is what Wahu refers to when she talks of the man's use of a "fake accent." One only needs to listen to young hip hop artistes being interviewed by foreign journalists about their music to see and hear the propensity of American slang in these young people's spoken English. Indeed, there is a joke among many Kenyans that when Kenyans go abroad to study, the ones who go to the United States and the United Kingdom come back with thick American and British accents, while those who go to India never do. This, of course, exemplifies the politics of speech and cultural referents where countries with higher economic and cultural statuses become positive markers of one's sociocultural identity. Wahu sings the last three lines excerpted above while emphasizing an American accent by placing on the sound "a," found in the words of the song, an American "r" sound that commonly differentiates British and American spoken English. This "r" sound is often used by East Africans who wish to sound American (or Americanized) because it bestows upon them a higher social status than their counterparts who may not have left East Africa.

This accent "pick-up" is also quite common among East African radio DJs, whether they have been to the West or not, because most of them seek to sound like their Western counterparts and may assume that such speech projection defines successful radio DJs. In presenting this man's appropriation of an American accent, Wahu is thus weaving into her song the reality of living in a former colonial locale that has complex notions of cultural inferiority and a desire to copy the West in order to elevate one's sociocultural standing. She also critiques the growing notion of "been there" that many youth crave in defining their cosmopolitan and modern identities. Many times, these opportunities are also gendered as there are more men traveling abroad than women. Consequently, men tend to have more encounters with foreign cultures that they can appropriate and use to enhance their social standing than do women.

(Re)Constructing Gender, Reshaping Values

To further understand how hip hop expresses gendered identities and how it mobilizes and shapes understanding of gender, an analysis of a few more songs by East African artistes, both male and female, will suffice. As stated above and also shown elsewhere (Ntarangwi 2003c), despite that few female popular musicians in East Africa hold dominant positions other than backup singers and dancers, the few that are there have produced important critiques of how gender is constructed and expressed in many social forums. Although one can see Wahu as an artist who frowns at the construction of women as "gold diggers," she does also show some consistency in challenging male perceptions of women as well as highlighting the consequential realities of poor life choices made by some women. This is the same strategy used by Zay B from Tanzania. Yet, hip hop and its construction or expression of gender spans a whole spectrum.

Dan Teng'o, who writes for a local Kenyan daily newspaper, notes that much of the hip hop music heard in East Africa comprises songs with topics that are "disturbingly trivial—alcohol, blind revelry and sexual promiscuity" with "few singers tackling constructive themes such as education, politics or social issues" (Teng'o 2003b). The immense popularity these songs enjoy, however, points to an audience thirsty for a local style of hip hop that is not laced with serious content. Interestingly, hip hop songs with serious social meanings such as Kalamashaka's "Ni Wakati" may not generate as much popularity as the "disturbingly trivial" songs such as "Ninanoki (I go crazy)" and "Teremuka (Get down)" by Kenya's Nameless and Deux Vultures, respectively. While the popularity of a song may depend on factors such as airtime on public radio, live performances, and marketing strategies used by artistes and producers, many more hip hop songs tackle constructive themes now than in the late 1990s. The hard-hitting lyrics in songs by groups such as Ukooflani Mau Mau are not played on radio as frequently as those with trivial messages. With increased avenues to channel the music including through the Internet, sale of pirated music, and at dance clubs, these artistes' popularity continues to grow. In the recent past, more and more songs with social messages are vigorously competing for prominence, and a number of them present critiques of gender.

Wahu again seems to have drawn quite a large following with her songs that present serious messages. Her songs "Liar," "Sitishiki," and "Kibow Wow" all discuss the problem of male-female relations, which are often based on deception and lack of social maturity. "Sitishiki (I am unshakable)" engenders a feminist critique of social realities that pit men against women in social relations involving love, money, and sexuality. The popularity of this song was evident to me when I witnessed Wahu perform it live at K1. Her words in the song are quite challenging as she confronts a man whose behavior she highly critiques:

> This man thinks he is a Casanova, this man thinks is an operator
> Showing off his expensive car, showing off his expensive house
> You have one problem, you think you can shake me
> I am unshakable . . .
> So you buy me a drink or two and expect me to go home with you
> Take a look at yourself, watch out you don't trip, sir

In an interview with Teng'o, Wahu says, "The song is about an emerging breed of women with good education and good jobs . . . who are breadwinners in their households, and head various national and international organizations" (quoted in 2003a). In this regard, Wahu is clearly projecting herself as a serious critic of male chauvinism and a voice for women who may not find many opportunities to assert and express their own experiences due to limited social outlets for such discourse. This is the same role she takes up in "Kibow Wow" in reference to a critique of a masculine identity built upon a false display of wealth. In this way, Wahu continues to present an alternative voice to an otherwise male-dominated and male-structured music arena. In her hit song *Liar,* Wahu again castigates men who are dishonest in their relationships by showing the naiveté that a woman could display when falling for a man based purely on his physical attributes. In the song, Wahu presents another important aspect of sexual relations but in a more nuanced and real way. She introduces us to sex and its dire consequences.

Sex and Its Consequences

One of the critiques against hip hop in East Africa today is its reckless presentation of sexuality. Sex and sexuality sell in every culture, and hip hop has been involved quite extensively in that project. The more racy a song is, the more popular it seems to be among its consumers. A few songs, however, present sex and sexuality in a more realistic and responsible way. They present not only the pleasures of sex but its consequences as well. This is important in a region that continues to have high incidents of and deaths from HIV/AIDS and unplanned pregnancies. In a classic feminist critique of romance and sexuality, Wahu uses "Liar" to state:

> He told me he loved me and that he would do anything to have me
> He told me he wanted to be the one who would make me happy
> I said to my mama, "Mama, I think I found him"
> And then mama told me, "Girl, you must have been silly, can't you see"
> He is a liar (his lovely eyes), a liar (his sexy smile)
> He is a liar but I was hypnotized by his lovely eyes and sexy smile
> Oh Oh, mama, what am I going to do?

The song presents the classic story of "girl meets boy," who get physically attracted to each other but without much probing take all the promises to heart, only to find out later that some caution and depth may have been necessary before going too far. It is not clear from the text what the full extent of the mother's advice was when the girl announced she had "found him." Ignoring what the mother said and thought, the girl must have entered into an intimate relationship with the man she met and ended up pregnant. One of the common characteristics of hip hop songs even in the United States is that when they promote a life of reckless abandon involving sex and drinking, they hardly show the dire consequences of such behavior. This is what makes Wahu's song very powerful. She not only presents the romance plot common in many hip hop songs but also articulates clearly the results/consequences of sexual unions that follow such plots. To add insult to injury, she presents the scenario when the woman finds herself in double jeopardy: pregnant and abandoned. The man responsible for the pregnancy denies any responsibility and calls her a liar. Wahu narrates this next part of the story:

> I woke up one morning feeling a little bit funny
> I went to the doctor and asked what was wrong with me
> The doctor told me, "There is no problem you will soon have a baby"
> I wrote a letter to my sweetie saying you will soon be a father
> A little bit later I heard a knock on the door
> And there stood my sweetie and this is all he had to say to me
> "You are a liar (how can I be sure), a liar (I am responsible)
> You are a liar (girl you must be wrong) ooh"

This part of the song features Wahu singing the woman's part while a man sings the words in brackets. The man accuses the woman of lying that he is responsible for the pregnancy. She had earlier accused him of lying to her and enticing her with his lovely eyes and sexy smile. This dual blaming seems to confirm Wahu's comments about the song's intended message that "it does not imply that only men are liars, anyone could be a liar in a relationship. It could be the man or the woman" (Teng'o 2003a). When the woman in the song finally realizes her predicament, she shares her insights on this bitter but inevitable learning process:

> Oh, mama, what am I going to do, what am I going to do now tell me
> He made me feel like a black Cinderella then a little later he dumps me
> I did not even know the fool had a wife at home
> If you see him before I do, just tell him he is a liar

Stories abound of young women who often find themselves in similar situations. Having gone through college in the years when most students in public universities continue to find it hard to juggle academic requirements with meager financial resources, Wahu is probably warning many young college students who might fall prey to dishonest men out to misuse them.[2] "Liar" is a song that situates itself as a platform for the negotiation of social and sexual relations in the context of Western tenets of romantic love that often tend to emphasize individual choices based upon physical attributes as well as self-stated commitments. This is in contrast to more-traditional relationships and unions in which one's parents are heavily involved in the choice of partner. In "Liar," Wahu presents the woman trying to avoid any interventions by the parent in the decision-making process. These romance-based sexual relations are much more a phenomenon of Wahu's generation than that of her mother, where choice of marriage partner was often shaped by collective, rather than individual, considerations. When she ends the song by stating, "I did not even know the fool had a wife at home," Wahu is also presenting a real scenario in much of East Africa where infidelity is a common practice. In Tanzania, for instance, it is common knowledge that many married men have mistresses, locally referred to as *nyumba ndogo* (small house). In Kenya and Uganda, the mistresses are called *ndogo ndogo* (small ones) and *naku* (the name of an alleged mistress of a senior politician).

Tanzania's hip hop artiste Zay B presents a slightly different scenario in her song "Monica." Instead of a man enticing the naïve woman into a reckless lifestyle as Wahu's *Liar* does, Zay B's "Monica" presents a scenario in which a fellow woman is the villain. "Monica" places the blame of the predicaments faced by women on women themselves and also reestablishes the important role parents play in shaping the lives of youth in contemporary East Africa. There is a growing tendency among many East African youth, just as it is among their peers all over the world, to regard their elders as incompetent in today's world, where wisdom accumulated through lived experiences is sacrificed at the altar of technology and modernity. Zay B's song seems to challenge this perception as she shows what happens when a young woman ignores her parents' counsel to stay in school and avoid bad company. In "Monica," Zay B starts by singing

> I was quiet people called me the pious one
> In school I was praised for good behavior
> I did not expect to encounter bad company that led me astray
> I became hard-headed and didn't care about school
> I was so bad when I got a zero in my tests I thought I was hot
> I was proud of my beauty, my parents warned me but I ignored them
> We started going astray and never quite recovered, me and my
>   friend Monica

Once she befriended Monica, her life took a different turn; it became a life of sexual promiscuity and recklessness:

> Trouble started like a joke, I did not know Monica was so loose
> Her life involved dating wealthy older men
> Whenever we went somewhere, she would leave me with her
>   man's friend
> He too had his own plans but I didn't know this yet
> So when he came onto me, I was scared and kept my distance
> When I told Monica about it, she told me
> "Why are you playing with your luck?"
> Then I told her that I was scared
> "Scared of what, grow up!"
> What if my father found out?
> "Who will tell him? Look here, there are many girls who want this man
> He is rich and even has a car, we will always get rides
> Go out with him, don't waste this opportunity"
> It is not a secret Monica convinced me and I started going out
>   with the man

The same trappings of money that lead young women into the arms of older men are what Zay B presents as the cause of the troubles that befalls the character she plays in this song. This phenomenon is common in the region, and "Monica" is a reflection of social reality. A recent report by UNICEF shows that 30 percent of girls aged between twelve and eighteen in Kenya, for instance, were engaged in casual sex for money (2006). Just as in the case of Zay B's narrative in "Monica," the UNICEF report gives an example of one of the interviewees: "[L]ike many other teenagers in Mtwapa, Annie was introduced to sex-for-cash by her peers. 'They told me I could earn money easily by simply having sex with men,' she says" (2006).

The report continues that 75 percent of men interviewed and those who were involved in the tourism industry itself thought it was acceptable for girls to exchange sex for cash (2006). Many people interviewed also saw the sex industry as the only way of putting food on the table. In Tanzania, research by Tanzania Media Women Association (TAMWA) shows that poverty and sexual abuse at home are among some of the factors driving more and more Tanzanian children into the sex industry.[3] With so many people living below the poverty line in East Africa,[4] Zay B's song is not a compilation of words that rhyme—it is very much part of the reality of many young women in East Africa and beyond. As in the song "Liar" by Wahu, Zay B's "Monica" also presents the consequences of a reckless lifestyle. Zay B continues to narrate the story of Monica's friend:

> It started with nausea and vomiting
> I went to the hospital and the doctor said I was pregnant
> I was kicked out of home and then went to my man
> But he chased me away like I was a dog
> I wished the ground would break open and swallow me whole
> I did not know what to do so I went to Monica who told me
> "You are hilarious, are you afraid of just one pregnancy?
> I have had more than eleven abortions
> Don't worry, I will give you some pills
> Once you get rid of it, we will resume our happy life"

This song is performed in the classic style of dialogue and storytelling that is quite prominent in East Africa and other parts of Africa. Zay B takes the role of the affected narrator who uses her experiences to warn young people of the consequences of bad company and the choices they make in life. The refrain or chorus in the song becomes the knell that seals the fate of this reckless lifestyle. It states that Monica led her astray, and now she is lying in her deathbed. Zay B says in the song that when she took the pills to aid in the abortion, she had an out-of-body experience, came face to face with the angel of death, and wished she had listened to her parents. Such dire consequences faced by this young woman tell of the dangers that face many girls growing in poverty who are yet enticed by the flashy urban lifestyle of money and fun. Because abortion is illegal in East Africa, many young women go through unsafe abortions that lead to health risks and complications (Rogo 1993; Rasch 2003; Singh et al. 2005). Even though both Zay B and Wahu talk of contemporary forms of gender realities, other artistes present a very different version of such reality, opting to push for essentialized notions of gender.

Tradition and Modernity in Gendered Identities

Unlike Wahu and Zay B, Uganda's Jose Chameleone constructs a different scenario of gender relations by presenting a case of a jilted lover and husband. In the song "Mama Mia," Chameleone complains that he has been left by his spouse, Njoki, because she is still physically attractive. Chameleone laments,

We have had eight children together
Now you leave me saying you are tired and that I am poor
Now you discard me, where do I go, what do I do?
The kids are crying at home, but that is life
You seek pleasure first, ignoring me, Njoki
Why did you leave, leaving me with eight children?
They are still crying at home, Njoki, why did you leave me?
It is because you have a bottle-shaped figure

The theme of physical attributes and material possessions seems to run through not only hip hop songs but also most songs regarding male-female relations in East Africa. Other musical genres such as *taarab* and *kadongo kamu* tend to present similar themes (see, for instance, Nannyonga-Tamusuza 2002 and Ntarangwi 2003c). The theme of poverty is further explored in Chameleone's song:

I am your lover don't leave me saying that I am poor
Beware that those with Mercedes-Benz cars have the money
Yet they have no love and that is the truth
Chameleone is the true lover don't leave me saying that I am poor
Beware that those with BMW cars have money and yet no love
The world is full of surprises, even men cry

Chameleone addresses two issues that are unusual in the public construction of masculine identity in much of East Africa in "Mama Mia." First, the scenario in which a man admits publicly he is crying and wants his wife back is an interesting phenomenon within the East African cultural context. Part of masculine identity for many East African males is the idea that public display of emotion such as crying is unwelcome. Few are the cases in public discourse, if any, in which men admit crying because of being abandoned by a woman. The expectation that "men don't cry" very much defines the received norm of masculine identity in much of East Africa. Second, rare are the cases of women who leave their husbands with eight children. It is mostly men who leave women with children and with no child support. In this case, therefore, Chameleone is portraying a man as the victim of domestic disdain and the woman as the villain. It creates a good contrast for reading Wahu's song "Liar" in which the woman was attracted to a man who later abandoned her when she became pregnant. While the image of gender as constructed in Chameleone's song above is the exception rather than the rule, it allows for an alternative imagining of gender relations in the contemporary era inhabited by these artistes.

Another Ugandan musician, Mesach Ssemakula, presents another case of gender relations that reverses the masculine role of the strong leader and uplifts the role of the woman as the one in charge of the household and relationship. In his song "First Aid," Ssemakula acts as the smitten husband who wishes his wife could spend more time with him. In the video version of the song, the man, played by Mesach, fakes illness so that his wife, who is a nurse, can attend to him. When she ends up leaving him at home to go to work, he follows her to the hospital and pretends to be sick, collapsing in the doctor's office. When the doctor examines him and realizes that the man really is faking it, he writes a "prescription" for him that he hands to the nurse, who is also the "patient's" wife. The prescription reads, "Give your husband more time, he is not sick." When they go back home, the man is again shown as incapable of keeping a job because he is always thinking about his wife. He is fired, and when he tries his hand at housework, the audience sees a man who cannot cook, breaks plates, and burns food. He is simply helpless without her.

These alternative representations of gendered identities are, however, being challenged by a revitalization of traditional gender values as seen in Lady JayDee's song discussed here below. Lady JayDee, from Tanzania, became famous in East Africa for her song "Wanaume Kama Mabinti (Men who are like women)," in which she castigates men who have literally become feminized as seen through their public behavior. She sings in the refrain,

> You eat, drink, and get clothed day in day out
> You like to get things for free and you don't care
> You fit in every side as days go by
> You are full of gossip, men who have become like women

The ideology that places men and women in two separate and distinct social categories is a common phenomenon among many African indigenous cultures. To imagine a gender identity that is not dichotomous is to step out of the social norm. Lady JayDee's song challenges such an imagining by redrawing traditional gender lines that place men and women in separate social worlds and categories. The men represented in this song seem unabated by the fact that they are not economically independent but are constantly being supported. To further show their feminization, these men also display traits such as gossip that are associated with women. Lady JayDee is quick to note that she does not refer to all men but to those who act like women:

When I say men, I do not mean all of them
But those with traits similar to those of women
You will see them in their girlfriend's cars
Smiling and laughing you would think they are really something
They like to soothe older women and endear them
Yet they have no genuine love but are constantly thinking about money
If I say they sell themselves, I will not be wrong
What is the difference between them and prostitutes?

This part of Lady JayDee's song is interesting when compared to Chameleone's song above that castigates Njoki for chasing after wealthy men and who have no genuine love. Lady JayDee similarly castigates men who go after older women for their money and thus displaying no genuine love but still want to be supported by their girlfriends.

Chapter 1 shows how changes in the East African economy have affected the lives of many people. This has ramifications visible in all sectors of life and that lead to the kinds of individual practices being highlighted here by Lady JayDee. These men seem to have no problem being supported economically. As Lady JayDee shows,

If you meet them in beerhalls, they are the know-it-all type
Yet they will not contribute a cent towards paying the bar bill
When it's their turn to buy beer, they go to the toilet
They are tricky and cunning
They like to entertain their friend's girlfriends
My friends, please bring on some dresses we dress them up
Bring headscarves we tie on them plus some miniskirts to lend
    to these men

The ultimate step is to physically turn these "parasitic" men into women by making them dress up like women. Lady JayDee is questioning these men's masculinity because of engaging in "female behavior." In so doing, she projects a dichotomized view of gender in which men have specific identities that clearly separate them from those of women, and any conflation of such distinct roles is unwelcome. Indeed, as she states at the end of the song, "Where have you seen a man who is always bought beer? Since when did a real man braid his hair?"

As many hip hop artistes continue to take their public image cues from their counterparts in the United States, they have had to confront the challenges of local perceptions and realities of gendered identity and the global projections of modernity. A number of East Africa males have copied hair-styles emanating from the United States (see Weiss 2002), and this has created a heated debate even on Internet listservs by East Africans (see Ntarangwi 2007). Braiding, dyeing, and straightening hair are practices exclusively associated with females, and men who do so quite often draw the wrath of the public and even family members. Braiding is only an accepted practice for men when it is a cultural tradition as practiced by pastoralists in East Africa such as the Maasai, Samburu, and Rendille. The identities of modernity and transculturation being mobilized by hip hop such as hair braiding for men become targets of criticism from hip hop artists themselves, even though they use the same facets of this modernity to define themselves.

Bobi Wine's song "Adam ne Kawa (Adam and Eve)" takes these differences between men and women to another level by showing that they are not only clearly visible but also divinely defined. Bobi Wine makes reference to the Judeo-Christian creation story of Adam and Eve and says in the song that

> Some things in this world are the way they are, because they were
> meant to be so
> God knows because as the creator He made them husband and wife
> And each one of them has a role to perform
> The man is in charge and the wife obeys him
> That way the home stays in harmony
> This was started by our great grandparents, Adam and Eve
> And that is how it shall be, now and forever

Many artistes use religion to explain the way men and women are to relate to each other as well as their traditional roles. Lady JayDee's expectations of a "real" man even though not couched in religion seems quite in line with Bobi Wine's. To her, a "real man" includes such qualities as supporting himself economically and avoiding "female" practices such as braiding hair. For Bobi Wine, to imagine a different gender arrangement is to step outside of the will of God. This is a very familiar discourse in many cultures as traditional structures and institutions such as family and marriage continue to be challenged by new experiences and ideologies. This shows that while we may celebrate the fact that hip hop has opened up some spaces to contest conservative views of women, it has also allowed for the reinscription of those views.

There are other times when women have been depicted in the stereotypical manner in which their beauty is central in their relations with men. This seems to be another predominant motif that has made many hip hop artistes in East Africa quite popular. In his song "Manzi wa Nairobi (Nairobi girl)," Kenya's Nonini says

> In the entire world no other girl matches the one from Nairobi
> She adorns herself well and her clothes are spotless
> You will always see her walking in town with a swagger
> If she walks past you, you will definitely turn around
> If I were judge, the Miss Universe pageant would be easy
> All Nairobi girls would win quite easily

While this song can be interpreted as representing a male gaze on a female body, it is also a commentary on the mode of dress that often separates people of different generations. Through Westernization and its resultant culture of hip hop, East African youth have adopted a style of dress where young men and women dress up like hip hop stars seen on MTV and Channel O. The internationalization of this identity leads Nonini to declare that if he were the judge, Nairobi girls would be crowned Miss Universe all the time, pointing to a desire to localize the international beauty standards.

Deux Vultures's song "Mona Lisa" (discussed below), similar to Nonini's "Manzi wa Nairobi," focuses on the physical beauty of an urban woman. While the song is provocatively titled "Mona Lisa" to show a heightened global consciousness, it is situated within local sensibilities of beauty. The song is mostly rendered in Sheng but uses some Spanish and French words to complete the cosmopolitanism sought after by many hip hop groups in East Africa. The song introduces this extra ordinary woman:

> It's dawn and I am awake
> I pass through Mama Ngina [street], I hear coo coo doo doo
> Take this, after a short while I see a pretty girl
> Expensive kind of you would think she just landed
> Let me tell you, she had on a black stretcher
> A blue silky top and a pair of black sketchers
> An African queen, a rare kind of species that none of you has ever seen

This Mona Lisa girl is really an extraordinary woman with a cosmopolitan identity that requires sophisticated reference points for identity. Mona Lisa in its original context refers to a painting by Italian artist Leonardo da Vinci that was started in 1503 and finished three or four years later. The painting depicts a portrait of a woman of European descent wearing an introspective expression and smiling slightly. The original painting has hung in the Louvre Museum in Paris since the mid-1500s when the artist visited France. It is probably the most famous portrait in art history and has been reproduced and reshaped to fit many different contexts and styles. The current rendition of Mona Lisa in Deux Vultures's song is yet another addition to this myriad process of localizing international notions of beauty in ways that are reproduced to fit specifically desired images and identities.

This discussion of beauty and identity using references that reach out beyond the local seems to reveal a seemingly global consciousness. For instance, in Wahu's song "Liar" as well as Deux Vultures's "Mona Lisa," there is mention of a Black Cinderella and an African Queen, respectively, and Nonini's song talks of a possible Miss Universe title for the Nairobi girl. All these inferences show a regional or global consciousness in which life and identities imagined and mobilized through hip hop music in East Africa draw on both the local and global (Remes 1998). The artistes and their audience members are not confined to a local realm of imagined existence but are rather opened to the various Western forms of identities mobilized through hip hop and at the same time acknowledging its local roots. It is thus instructive that the song presents Mona Lisa as an African Queen who is famous for her ability to wiggle her body (unlike the original Mona Lisa who is only depicted from chest upwards and shows little emotional expression).

What has emerged in my analysis so far is the congruence of themes, symbols, and meanings articulated by East African artistes in reference to the wide field of gender. The centrality of material wealth in defining gendered relationships, the discussion of the role of parents in romantic plots, and the redrawing of gender boundaries in the face of conflated femininity and masculinity all point to the vibrant social world inhabited and imagined by East Africa's youth. It is a world in which their own aspirations and experiences become entangled in the images and realities of a modernity produced by colonialism, Westernization, and globalization. In the process, the youth construct a local modernity that enables them to inhabit two worlds—the global and the local—simultaneously. Yet, this is also a world subject to other powers, both economic and political, that belong to a world beyond their immediate locale or influence. This is the subject that forms the discussion engaged in the next chapter.

4

Economic Change
and Political Deception

Juma's mother! Come, there is something I would like to tell you
You know the general elections are nearing
And many are the candidates who want my seat
I don't want to let go of my seat
Even though I have not fulfilled my promises to the electorate
I don't know who will assist me so that I can stay in power . . .
I think only an herbalist can assist you, my husband

—John Woka and Ras Lion, "Tawire," part 1

Multiparty Politics and Deceptive Politicians

Scholars and students of East African politics reveal the complexity and fragility of the state, especially in response to democratic principles and accountability to its masses. For some scholars, it is clear that democratization in much of Africa is completely detached from the lives of people (Joseph 2003), as many leaders are engaged in the politics of accumulation and distribution of state resources mostly for personal enhancement (Bayart 1993) as well as a reflection of the global political realities of the neoliberal economic agenda (Joseph 1998). As politicians grapple with the reality of their own powerlessness within larger global structures, they focus inwards to local resources and how to use them strategically to remain in power. For many of these politicians, politics is an opportunity for self-aggrandizement and will do anything to get into and stay in power. They will make all manner of promises to the electorate and present themselves as the most deserving leaders or even consult supernatural powers as the song excerpted above indicates.

In the 1997, political campaigns for a parliamentary seat in a constituency next to my own in Meru, Eastern Kenya, one political candidate promised his constituents that they would get electricity if they voted for him in the upcoming elections. When elections results were announced and the candidate realized he had lost, he went back to the constituency the next day and collected all the electricity poles that he had earlier taken to a local school as proof of his campaign promises. One only needs to pick up a local daily newspaper during an election year in any of the East African countries and find numerous reports of political aspirants promising their electorate all manner of goodies in order to be elected. This is a very common practice in many parts of East Africa because political power denotes access to material goods that are subsequently used to build an individual politician's support base. It is common practice for political candidates to not only give unattainable promises to the electorate but also repackage themselves to project the best public image. In the 2006 general elections in Uganda, for instance, most candidates had artists brush up and reconstruct their photographs that were used in campaign posters so that they looked much younger than they really were. This was a strategy by older politicians seeking to endear themselves to a youthful population in Uganda that was increasingly asking for fresh ideas in their political leadership and had the numbers to make a political difference. Both these scenarios can explain why John Woka and Ras Lion's song excerpted above is an important allegory of political culture in East Africa.

A casual observation of East Africa's political terrain reveals that majority of politicians are over fifty years old, and even though many subscribe to the rhetoric of youth as the leaders of tomorrow, very little youth engagement in East African politics is visible. There are few, if any, opportunities for youth to fully participate in the political process in much of East Africa despite that they constitute more than half of the entire population (Barkan 2004). Politics continues to be dominated by the older generation and quite often amongst a handful of cronies. This anomaly has become a major part of youth discourse through hip hop as they debate their role in the emerging political changes, especially those brought about by multiparty politics that emerged in the early 1990s. When I visited with Tanzania's hip hop artiste Professor Jay (Joseph Haule) in Dar es Salaam in 2006, he mentioned the overall frustration that many youth have with politics and politicians in Tanzania. He felt that many of the serving politicians did not truly represent their constituents, because there wasn't much of a public discussion of matters affecting individuals and communities represented.

Professor Jay is well-known in East Africa because his music centers on socially conscious messages. In 2001, for instance, his song "Ndio Mzee," which criticizes politicians who make unattainable promises to the electorate just to get voted into parliament, became a hit in East Africa. As Professor

Jay told me, he had to be careful not to release the song before Tanzania's general elections in 2000 lest it was hijacked by politicians from both ends (government and opposition).[1] Even though Professor Jay had been quite vocal in presenting the plight of the poor, especially the youth, while he was performing with the group Hard Blasters, "Ndio Mzee" was the song that undoubtedly established him as a serious social critic. I remember hearing a lot of Tanzanians in Arusha in September of 2001 talking animatedly about the song and its social relevance. At the time, I was leading a group of American undergraduate students on a study tour into Northern Tanzania. Some of the local guides we had on the trip would frequently sing the song and debate amongst themselves how well the song articulated the reality of politics in Tanzania. I had a chance to listen to the song on radio one day and was quite taken by the lyrics. I wanted to hear more of it and other songs by the artiste. I asked our local Tanzanian guides where I could find it, and they suggested I look for it in downtown Arusha. Unfortunately, I did not get a chance to go through downtown Arusha on our way back to Kenya from northern Tanzania, so I decided to look for the song in Namanga (a border town between Kenya and Tanzania). Every vendor I asked told me it was sold out even on the Kenyan side. It was not until a month later that I was able to purchase the song's entire album in a music store in Nairobi's River Road area.

When I listened to many songs on the album, I soon realized why Professor Jay's "Ndio Mzee" had drawn animated discussions among the local Tanzanian guides with whom we had worked. The song narrated scenarios of political culture in Tanzania that were very similar to what I had experienced in Kenya. The song, shown below, is a political commentary that has relevance beyond its local confines. Professor Jay paints scenarios that allow the listener to see how politicians can promise unattainable things just to get elected. He takes on the role of the politician and presents a political speech at a public rally. From the issues that are raised in the song, it is evident that Professor Jay understands the East African political terrain and the particular issues that excite the electorate. This critical understanding of the politics of the day has won Professor Jay many local accolades. Indeed, his contribution to sociopolitical discourse in Tanzania has attained national importance.

During an interview at his home in Dar es Salaam, Professor Jay proudly told me that he was one of three Tanzanians honored by the government for contributing to social progress. He was specifically honored for sensitizing people on good governance.[2] Maybe the weight of this recognition can be clearly seen when we consider that the other two honorees were a former prime minister and an ambassador. That a young person, and a musician for that matter, was honored by his nation in the same rank with career politicians / civil servants is a testimony to the role of hip hop in contemporary Tanzanian society and Professor Jay's image as a social critic. As he told me, he was honored for *mada nzito* (serious themes) in his music and plans to remain a voice of reason for those who may not be able to publicly voice their experiences and concerns.

This chapter analyzes the work of artistes who critique politics and politicians and the way they interact with everyday experiences of many East Africans. Many of the songs studied here bring forth voices of frustration that are evident among many East Africans who, due to internal political mismanagement (Joseph 1998, 2003) and external structures of domination (Crowder 1987b; Mkandawire 2002), find their nations continually struggling economically and politically. As power and resources get restricted among very few people, many politicians have been forced to result to creative and at times disingenuous strategies to access power. As a result, they have pursued their own individual wants for self-aggrandizement or what Jean-Francois Bayart calls "politics of the belly" (Bayart 1993). Professor Jay's critique of the role played by politicians is found in "Ndio Mzee" because, as he explained to me, "Politicians want power for their own benefit, and the electorate support it by voting them in."[3] The song forcefully critiques politicians who selfishly use their political campaigns to promise the electorate unattainable things. At the beginning of the song, Professor Jay takes on the role of the political aspirant:

> Okay my name is Joseph Haule
> I think I have been brought to save this generation
> I am a politician blessed by God
> I have been brought to you to solve your problems
> I am the chosen one in Africa south of the Sahara
> That is why I was given the highest award for leadership
> I am better than King Solomon, so don't worry
> I will prove to you my abilities as soon as you elect me to parliament
> I will make Tanzania the strongest nation in the world

Increased joblessness, insecurity, economic and political anxieties, among many other challenges allow for this kind of political rhetoric to be condoned. Professor Jay takes on the role of the politician and promises to bring radical changes to Tanzania that will make it the strongest nation in the world. He goes on to give more promises:

I want to turn Tanzania into Europe
The first thing I will do is eradicate poverty
Students will do their science experiments on the moon
I will provide hospitals with as many drugs as there is sand in the sea
I will open bank accounts for every child
Faucets will flow with water and milk, all villagers will forget about
    dugout wells
I will sponsor experts to make planes
So that everyone can have one, including drivers and conductors

Professor Jay locates his satire on issues that are of critical importance to the welfare of all communities in East Africa—healthcare, education, water, and transportation—and, hence, touches on the nerve of people's expectations and needs. By claiming to turn Tanzania into Europe, he is reflecting the relationship that exists between colonial history and postcolonial aspirations of modernity. As shown in chapter 2, Europe and European culture play a critical role in the imagination and expression of contemporary East African modernity. Four decades after colonialism, many of the public institutions, such as education, religion and law, are still modeled after European ones, making it quite clear why Europe continues to be the yardstick by which to measure "development" in East Africa. Professor Jay continues his political campaign and makes even more promises:

I am amazed that civil servants have no vehicles
This is dangerous
I plan to increase your salaries, 100 times of what led you to
    go on strike
I will give you big houses and big cars, people will be amazed when
    they see you
I will give every farmer a tractor; I think that will aid the
    [agricultural] sector
You will sell billions worth of agricultural products
People will be amazed, their jaws will drop
As for teachers I have their treasures in my heart, just wait you
    will be delighted

This very careful choice of "benefits" to promise the electorate again represents Professor Jay's astuteness in capturing the very nature and tone of political campaigns not only in Tanzania but also in the entire East African region. Making promises of personal gains such as getting personal vehicles for civil servants and tractors for farmers resonates with the individual aspirations of many East Africans, not to mention the benefits politicians them-selves get. In Kenya, for instance, members of parliament make more than US$150,000 a year besides medical insurance, car loan, and travel allowance. These tangible financial benefits make going to parliament such a coveted opportunity that in the recently concluded 2007 elections, some constitu-encies had up to forty-five candidates vying for a single parliamentary seat. Professor Jay further articulates this clamor for power by introducing even more political promises:

> By the way I give praise to all police officers
> The way you apprehend criminals is really commendable
> I plan to give each one of you a helicopter
> I think you've never dreamed of that
> Tanzanian citizens will never have to lock their houses
> In fact I will take control of crime

Many scholars have written about the criminalization of the state in Africa (Anderson 2002; Bayart, Ellis, and Hibou 1999; Joseph 1998;) and the resul-tant consequences of vigilantes and lawlessness (Anderson 2002). There are numerous examples of such scenarios in East Africa as evident in the plight of many Ugandans in Gulu under the menace of the Lord's Resistance Army (LRA), Tanzania's political violence in 2001 and 2005 especially in Zanzibar, and Kenya's postelection violence in 2008 and the continued challenges of the *Mungiki*—a quasi-political religious group that is both a destructive cult and a criminal gang.

Of course, all the promises given by political candidates, as presented by Professor Jay, often come to naught once the candidate makes it to par-liament. This reality is not lost to Professor Jay, who in his song "Kikao cha Dharura (Emergency meeting)," shows further political maneuvering through a review of the candidates first term in parliament. The song starts with the politician, again played by Professor Jay, wondering why he was called to an emergency meeting:

> Thank you, fellow citizens, for voting for me
> I am surprised I have been called to this emergency meeting
> The meeting indicates there're questions I need to address
> This must be related to "yes, sir" [Ndio Mzee] and my life
> I see there are a lot of people of great worth here today
> I am trying to figure out what could be the problem this time

The politician seems surprised that he has been called to a meeting by the electorate instead of regarding it as an opportunity to connect with his constituents. His surprise, as we learn through the song, is because he has not been able to meet all the promises he made during his political campaigns. The song is presented in a way that allows for the electorate to have a question-and-answer session with its representative. One of the members of public in the gathering says to this member of parliament, "I am Sergeant Philomena asking on behalf of the police force, could you tell us what became of the helicopters you promised us?"

The parliamentarian responds:

> I plan on starting a training college for pilots
> Otherwise you will have accidents in the air
> If right now you can't ride bicycles, how would you really
>   operate helicopters?
> Besides if everyone had a helicopter in the air, what would happen?

One may wonder why the politician had not thought of all these issues before making the initial promises. Yet, there is truth in assuming that the goal and essence of the initial promises were to get votes and that the politician may have had no claims or desire to articulate reality or truth.

Regarding promises made to farmers, someone asks him what happened, and he responds:

> Farmers should continue using the hand hoe
> The government has no money and the national budget has
>   been overstretched
> But I also see that hand cultivation is thriving
> So please keep working harder and toughen your muscles

It is common for many politicians to go back on their promises because of the realities surrounding fiscal operations of any government but especially those in regions such as East Africa where nations struggle to meet the needs of the majority of their population living in poverty. Confronted with the limits of government resources and unfulfilled campaigns promises, the politician has had to defend his discernible lack of accountability. When asked what happened to the promise of "taps running with milk across the country," he says:

> Please ask mature questions
> There is no way we can have taps flowing with milk and water
> You mis-reported me! I insist this is impossible

Here again Professor Jay demonstrates his ability to capture the reality of a politician's public life. Many politicians often engage in doublespeak, saying one thing now and another later. They are also quite fond of changing their positions depending on anticipated political consequences. Accusing the audience members of misreporting him allows the politician to shift the blame to others in order to still remain a viable candidate for another term in office. Regarding the promises he made to civil servants, he says:

> Why do civil servants need vehicles?
> There are so many public transport vehicles that you can ride to work
> I think that you love luxury more than work
> That is why you are ruining this generation

Granted that it would be a positive step for many civil servants to use public transportation because it would reduce undue stress on the environment than if they all drove personal vehicles. Yet. by making this statement the politician is insincere because he is not offering to use public transportation and also because he made the promise of personal vehicles to the civil servants.

Finally, someone in the audience asks about the promise he made about students conducting their science experiments on the moon. He responds:

> I promised students they will conduct their experiments on the moon
> But before I took them there, I did some research
> I found out that it's too cold on the moon
> There are also threats of there being Osama's camps
> If you elect me again, I will go there early enough
> Then I will fulfill every promise I have made
> Basically I have been pressed for time
> If you extend my time, everything will be fulfilled

The last two lines in this verse reveal that the politician is seeking a second term in order "to fulfill all his promises." Why should he be reelected when he unashamedly explains all his unfulfilled promises away by giving outrageous reasons? What will make him better in fulfilling his promises this time around? Having produced this song during the heat of "war on terror," Professor Jay is able to invest in the song words that reflect the international nature of terrorism. He gives his song this international flavor without losing his ability to understand and present the precarious relationship that exists between the electorate and their leaders. This relationship can be best understood if we interrogate political structures and practices not only in

East Africa but also in much of the continent. As Ian Taylor explains, "[P] ower in African politics must be generally understood as the utilization of patronage and not as the performance of legitimacy drawn from the sovereign will of the people. In other words, in spite of the façade of the modern state, power in most African polities progresses informally, between patron and client along lines of reciprocity. It is intensely personalized and is not exercised on behalf of the public good" (2004, 29).

This power arrangement exercised by African leaders in which they personalize state machinery is, as Michael Crowder argues, "an extension of the colonial state in which the Governor ruled by decree . . . [and] enjoyed to the full the outward trappings of power, living in an imposing palace, driven in large limousines flying the flag" (1987b, 15). African leaders inherited a corrupt political system that they have been unable to transform due to structures that defy quick fixes. Indeed, Jennifer Hasty describes, "the forms of desire that fuel corruption are not merely private but social" (2005, 271). The specific sociocultural contexts of power and privilege that enhance corruption also come with responsibilities and obligations at both the personal and collective levels. This power structure is reflective of the democratization process in Africa, which, Richard Joseph states, "is losing its connection with real lives of African people" (2003, 160) not because the leaders do not care but because they serve within larger, constraining global structures. Many politicians are thus caught up in this double bind—sociality that expects individuals in power to share resources with those closest to them and the reality of the scarcity of such resources. With the political role still a lucrative one for those who make it, some politicians started using and appropriating youth in ways that hardly benefit the youth.

Politics and the Appropriation of Youth Bodies

In a desperate search for a winning formula for its perennial political misfortunes, the opposition and even incumbent political establishments in Kenya have continually resorted to the support of youth to deliver victory for a team always mobilized as the change agents and savior of the political rot that continues to engulf the country's postindependence political structure. Thus, for instance, in an effort to oust a twenty-four-year Moi regime in 2002 following ten years of spirited efforts by an opposition created through multiparty politics, the National Rainbow Coalition (NARC), led by Mwai Kibaki, found a political anthem by appropriating the song "Unbwogable." Later and within a context of failed promises and the dishonoring of a memorandum of understanding between the founding members of the NARC group and the incumbent Kibaki government, the year 2005 saw another spirited effort to make political change when there was a referendum to decide on a new constitution for the country. The government was in support of a draft constitution, while other politicians, especially those aligned to the disenfranchised group that was sidelined by the Kibaki government, were against the new constitution. The opposing group formed the Orange Democratic Movement (ODM) that became a coalition of political parties in the 2007 general elections. In the referendum for a new constitution, two camps emerged that were symbolically represented by the Orange (those opposed and those who were members of ODM) or the Banana (those in favor and mostly those in government). The referendum became a tug-of-war between Oranges and Bananas, and in an effort to mobilize youth support, the Orange camp often used hip hop music to draw youth pursuing a new political destiny. A number of upcoming musicians were encouraged and even inspired to write and produce songs about the new wave of political dispensation that pitted the Orange group against the government's Banana group.

In early 2006, the incumbent government, through the office of public communication and government's spokesperson, again used youth and music to elicit nationalism and patriotism. The office sponsored a national music competition dubbed *Najivunia kuwa Mkenya* (I am proud to be Kenyan) aimed at encouraging the use of music as a platform to articulate youth patriotism. Numerous hip hop songs were performed, and new talents unearthed. The winner of the contest took home 100,000 Ksh. (Kenyan shillings) (about US$1,400) and a recording contract. On June 3, 2006, at a much-publicized rally, Narc-Kenya (a new political offshoot of NARC) was launched by drawing on youth through high-energy hip hop music as well as presenting itself as a party of the future. While the youngest of the politicians present, Danson Mungatana, can be considered to represent the youth, the rest of the politicians were all either from the past regime or in the president's age group. There are numerous other examples of this political appropriation of youth and music.

That the new political movements use the youth to mobilize support and create hopes of the future is very instructive. The youth has been identified both as a large political mass that can bring instant political change and also as a vulnerable group that can be easily exploited and appropriated for selfish political gains. In Kenya, the youth constitute not only a large majority but also a very vulnerable section of the population. Estimates from statistics available from the U.S. Central Intelligence Agency's *World Factbook* show that the youth (ages thirteen to thirty) constitute between 40 percent and 60 percent of the total population in Kenya.[4] Because the youth are heavily unemployed and always left out of any meaningful political participation, any opportunity to have access to political power that could subsequently improve their material fortunes is sought after and always welcome. Official (conservative) statistics state that out of 14.6 percent of unemployed persons in Kenya, the youth constitute 45 percent (Government of Kenya 2003, 8). Many of these unemployed youth become vulnerable and easily manipulated by promises of power and material gain or even access to it. Politicians understand this vulnerability and greatly exploit it.

The youth themselves have recently begun to appropriate hip hop music to make some political strides. In June 2006, for instance, I attended a youth political rally in Nairobi's Kamukunji Grounds, where many young people announced their intentions to vie for political office, with some of them specifying local civic seats they were going to contest in the 2007 elections in Kenya. The meeting had been organized and promoted as a free hip hop concert featuring local musicians and comedians. In between hip hop performances by such artistes as Ukooflani Mau Mau and Rufftone were short speeches by young political aspirants who urged the young crowd to acquire national identity cards and register as voters so that they could actually vote for their own candidates. Each speaker kept reminding the crowd that they were tired of being called *viongozi wa kesho* (tomorrow's leaders). This statement was met with a lot of cheering and ululation. The positive outcome of this promise is a welcome gesture in a political context of failed promises and self-absorbed politicians. Yet, the youth have little, if any, economic power that, in turn, makes their political participation weak, as they often tend to be led or manipulated by politicians with more economic power. There are a few examples of successful young politicians who contest seats on the strength of youth affairs and win or who by virtue of their political activities get nominated to political office. I am here thinking of Amina Chifupa, who was nominated to parliament on the strength of her fight against illegal drugs in Tanzania. Unfortunately, she passed away on June 26, 2007, at the age of twenty-six. In Kenya, Cecily Mbarire (age thirty), Amina Abdalla (thirty-three) and Njoki Ndung'u (thirty-seven) were the youngest members of parliament to be nominated in 2003.

One might concede that the youth have always been a part of the social changes going on in their societies and that participating in national politics is but another testimony of some adaptations to such changes. In that sense, the youth can be seen as willingly entering this political arena and participating through choice, and that such a choice is devoid of any political manipulation and appropriation. Yet, the appropriation of youth in the many phases of political processes in Kenya cannot be ignored. In 1992, the youth were appropriated by Youth for KANU '92 or simply YK '92, a moribund grouping of the then-ruling party KANU (the political Party Kenya African National Union). YK '92 was formed to counter the emerging multiparty political culture that spelled doom for KANU. Realizing the power of numbers and the vulnerability that comes with powerlessness, KANU manipulated the youth through strategies that made youth assume they would participate actively in the new phase of Kenyan politics. They were lured in with promises of material prosperity and often used to disrupt political gatherings and intimidate opposition politicians (Kagwanja 2005).

At the end of it all, the youth tend to always come out empty handed. The Moi and Kibaki governments have been accused of using the youth to mobilize the majority of their supporters but then quickly forgetting them as the leaders settled into their "old boys" club and appointed their friends and age mates into positions of power (Murunga and Nasong'o 2007). Granted that the Kibaki government sprinkled a few young people into positions of power, including Dr. Alfred Mutua as government spokesperson, Alfred Gitonga as the president's personal assistant, and Isaiah Kabira as head of the presidential press unit. In 2005, the government made an important move to create the Ministry of State for Youth Affairs and appointed young members of parliament, Dr. Mohamed Kuti (forty-two years old) and Katoo Ole Metito (thirty-two), as minister and assistant minister, respectively. These are laudable steps but with a large percentage of Kenya's population comprising the youth, the government should do even more to include them in political and economic affairs.

In economies such as those in East Africa, where there are not enough resources to meet the majority of the population's basic needs, this structure of political deception and manipulation becomes even more pronounced as politicians become the primary controllers of national resources. Such a system gets expressed in the most mundane areas of life and yet pervades every aspect of public and private life in East Africa. As shown in the preceding chapters, economic practices in East Africa have been negatively affected by the now dominant neoliberal agenda of reducing the role of government and increasing the role of the "market" as the key player in economic matters and resource management. For East African countries that were already unable to meet the basic needs of their citizens a decade after independence, privatizing social services increases the number of those in dire economic need

and expands the gap between the haves and have-nots, subsequently perpetuating a patron-client structure in the politicoeconomic arena. Many are
forced to seek alternative means of livelihood, including seeking indigenous
(traditional) health services as privatized healthcare becomes unattainable
and when government-supported healthcare crumbles. Others, for lack of
employment, enter into the unstable world of self-employment, especially
as vendors of consumer products that almost always are dumped into the
local market through the neoliberal market-driven economies. As I came to
understand during my field research, survival in such conditions requires
great ingenuity, even at some personal or community risk. Vendors in the
cities of Dar es Salaam, Kampala, and Nairobi have to continually negotiate
with or run away from city officials in order to avoid taxation or arrest for
contravening city bylaws that prohibit street vending.

When I arrived in Kampala in the morning of May 23, 2006, from Nairobi in an attempt to get the ground view of Uganda's hip hop scene, I was
accosted by many street vendors selling belts, shoes, and socks. I politely
turned down their offers and walked around in search of a foreign-exchange
bureau to change money. It had been four years since I had last been to
Kampala and although many physical places were quite familiar, a number
of things had changed. There seemed to be more people, more cars, and
many more motorbikes. I walked past the State House, the Sheraton Hotel,
and then came to the front side of the Grand Imperial Hotel, which occupies
a big piece of land in the better part of the city in which is housed a 103–
room hotel and mini shopping mall. The front-desk attendant at the hotel
I was staying in had suggested the Grand Imperial Hotel as a place I could
exchange U.S. dollars for local Uganda shillings. As I walked towards the
Grand Imperial Hotel's main entrance, I could see signs of foreign-exchange
booths announcing the daily exchange rates. I approached the structures
next to the signs and tried to compare the rates and hoping to get the best.
Two scouts, who I later came to learn worked for the forex bureaus, asked
me to visit their respective establishments, promising to give me the best
rate on my U.S. dollars.

The bureaus were next to each other, and I found it hard to decide which
one to go to so I just decided to go to the one closest to me. The scout who
invited me in said I would get a better rate than the one posted on the chalk-
board outside the stall. I was back into the signature East African culture of
haggling where nothing seems to have a fixed price. I went in and negotiated for a better rate just as the scout had mentioned and changed some U.S.
dollars into Uganda shillings. With local currency in my pocket, it was time

to have some lunch before going hunting for local music. I bought a local newspaper as well so that I could check for information on any live-music performances scheduled in Kampala. Through the years, I have learned to use this initial method of research to step into the local music scene. Local newspapers provide a context within which one can start asking questions and seeking local input. My subsequent visit in the summer of 2007 reflected similar trends, as I was able to learn of events in which artistes were launching new music or performing to a live audience.

One of the indicators of a country's economic strength is the value of its local currency against the U.S. dollar, although in 2007 and early 2008, the value of the U.S. dollar against other currencies was slowly dropping. In the case of Uganda at the time I was in Kampala in 2006, it took up to 1,840 Uganda shillings to get one U.S. dollar. In 2007, the Uganda shilling had gained strength and was changing at 1,640 for a U.S. dollar, yet this economic strength had not yet been actualized in local people's daily expenses, as many of them continue to struggle to make ends meet. Following the liberalization of the economy pushed by the International Monetary Fund (IMF) and the World Bank in the 1980s and 1990s, a new culture of competition, marketing, and manipulation was introduced in all sectors, both public and private, in Uganda. While competition may be healthy for the consumer in the short term, often offering a variety of products to choose from at competitive rates, there are very few real choices if businesses have to compete for imported items and services. The more liberal the economic structures in East Africa became, the fewer the number of local industries that survived the economic rollercoaster and the higher the rate of these nations' dependence on imported goods that subsequently led to the devaluation of the local currency.

A devalued local currency comes as an advantage for those, like me, who come into a country with stronger foreign currency such as the U.S. dollar or British pound. The power of the U.S. dollar, for instance, is apparent when dining in local restaurants and especially the ones that serve local cuisine. When I sat at the Slow Boat Restaurant in downtown Kampala and ordered for a mixed platter of chicken, *matooke* (cooked green bananas), *ugali*, rice, chapatti, and a glass of fresh passion juice, I paid $2.50. This price is still high for many Ugandans, who may not even make $2.50 a day. It all depends on social status and income level. For many of them, economic survival may entail small-scale business ventures such as motorbike taxis (locally known as *boda boda*), which symbolically reflect Uganda's economic status.

Of Boda Boda and Taxicabs

The numerous motorbikes that I noticed when I arrived in Kampala were boda boda. Boda boda had almost replaced the taxis that I had been used to taking to various destinations in the city. Boda boda were everywhere in the city and seemed to be doing a booming business, and unlike regular motorbikes, they have a slightly longer and more cushioned passenger's seat. They are operated by men and are often parked at corners of busy streets and even public markets as their operators keep a watchful eye for prospective clients and are quick to invite one to ride with them. Like many other transactions in East Africa, the cost of a boda boda ride is negotiable. One thing I noticed quickly about boda boda in Kampala was that they were not constrained by traffic jams or traffic lights and continually weaved around traffic to get the customer to his/her destination quickly. They also charged a fraction of what the regular taxis would charge. A trip to Makerere University on a regular taxi from the city center, for instance, was around US$4.00, while the same trip was US$0.80 on the boda boda.

Taking a boda boda for me was both quicker and economical, although it came with a number of challenges and risks. For starters, the passenger does not have a helmet or a comfortable support for his/her back, making the ride dangerous. Further, female clients have another challenge. Because the majority of women wear skirts and dresses, they have to sit across the seat with both legs dangling on the side of the motorbike away from the oncoming traffic and often risk falling off if the motorbike hits a large pothole or bump. With no good back support, helmet, or place to hold onto, this mode of transportation presents a real danger to passengers, but it provides a booming business for the owners.

The boda boda is a product of neoliberal economic strategies that define all transactions through prevailing market forces and are often unregulated by the state. By offering lower costs than regular taxis, the boda boda give their customers a comparable service for less money. Further, because they are able to maneuver through traffic faster, they have an advantage over regular taxis, which have to obey traffic rules. Their high numbers and availability at convenient points that can be accessed by most customers also gives them another edge over their competitors. The boda boda are almost irresistible because of these factors and explains why against my better judgment I took one to Makerere University in order to avoid the growing traffic jam. Given the way the motorbike cruised on the city streets with me in the passenger's seat, wearing no helmet and with nothing for support other than the seat I was sitting on, I knew I was in a compromising situation. I consoled myself by assuming that it was my way of "going native," because many local people used boda boda as their mode of transportation. I arrived at my destination safely but was still unsure if I wanted to take this risk once again. On my way back from Makerere, I decided to take a regular taxi.

When I got into the taxi, I heard a song on the radio that caught my attention specifically because of the lyrics that mentioned the need for East African unity. I asked the driver who the artiste was and where I could get the music. He told me it was a song by Bebe Cool and that I could get the music from a place called Wandegeya. I did not know where Wandegeya was but made a mental note to look for it later. I was interested in the song because the refrain stated that part of Africa's problems was a result of disunity. The singer kept saying that East Africans were not keen on working together and this contributed to their socioeconomic and political problems. The song seemed to fit into my research focus, especially on the reality of East African politics of geographic parochialism.

The next day, I went back to Makerere University to meet up with a few other people whom I had missed the previous day. Makerere University has an enduring history in East Africa and beyond. Some of the best-known African leaders and scholars were trained at Makerere. However, as I looked around the once-famous institution of higher learning, I noticed that much had changed. Some of the buildings were in poor physical state, with some wall paint peeling off and walls covered with all manner of flyers and posters. Heaps of trash were in many places within the university premises, and the notorious marabou storks were busy scavenging on them. It also seemed as if there were larger numbers of students than in previous years. Upon inquiry on campus, I learned that the university enrollment had increased to about thirty thousand from the usual ten thousand in the mid-1990s. A report by Makerere University's department of information and computing technology published in 2000 shows that the majority of these students (up to 80 percent) are private students paying their tuition and boarding fees directly, unlike the regular students who depend on government funding.[5]

This large student body had created opportunities for creative income-generating activities. I noticed many young people trying to make money by providing a variety of services to the university students. One young man stationed close to the main university gate was applying nail polish on numerous female students for a small fee. Another young man with a stapler was standing next to the Social Science Building making some money by stapling students' papers. It seemed as if economic liberalization had morphed into different forms of activities that affected different people variably. Increase in the demand for higher education and the subsequent withdrawal of government funding to public universities in keeping with the neoliberal agenda for economic restructuring have spelled doom for some Ugandans while availing numerous opportunities to others. It is common for those with disposable income to assume that stapling papers after photocopying is part of customer service but apparently not for a number of Makerere University students, many of whom were part of the expanded university enrollment that did not have a matching expansion in facilities and services. Such large numbers of students may lead to questions of quality and integrity, especially when student growth is not matched by faculty growth. Reports in local newspapers show that some students try to get better grades by offering sex to their professors. Some female students at Makerere University have been accused of sexually seducing their male teachers in exchange for better grades.[6] The same scenario has been reported for the University of Nairobi.[7] It seems like these are some of the results of a fast-changing society that are also noticeable in the proliferation of small businesses around the universities.

When I was done meeting with friends and contacts, I decided to walk to the small shopping center next to Makerere University where I could get a taxi to take me back to my hotel in Kampala. As I made my way to where the taxis were parked waiting for passengers, I noticed a large signboard stating that the market center ahead of me was Wandegeya. This was the place that the cabdriver who took me back to the hotel on my first day in Kampala had suggested I could find local music. I decided to look for some music before returning to my hotel. I walked into one of the stalls that was playing music, quite sure that someone in there would know where I could find local music. These stalls, as I soon realized, sold all kinds of items, from shoes to clothes and food, and were mostly run by youth. I assumed that this was a sign of youth entrepreneurial activities in an economy dominated by market forces. I decided to ask the two men I found in the stall where I could find local music. The stall was so small that only two people could fit in it at a time. The rest of the space was taken up by a large television, a computer, an amplifier, and empty boxes of blank compact disks. A small display case, which acted as the counter had about five recorded compact disks with a compilation of country-music songs.

"Where I can find local music by such artistes as Bebe Cool?" I asked one of the men. "Right here," he said looking up to face me. I could not hide my surprise. "Where is it?" I found myself asking in amazement. He told me to hold on as he finished selecting "best songs by Kenny Rogers" for the other man who turned out to be a customer. He was selecting songs from the computer and burning them onto a blank CD that he handed over to the customer. The customer gave him what I thought was about three thousand Uganda shillings (about US$1.10). Soon, a young woman came over, and both men got up to allow her to get into the stall. They stepped out of the stall, and she took the seat. I soon realized that she was the proprietor of the establishment. The man who was burning the Kenny Rogers music handed her the money he had been paid and told her that I was interested in some local music. She introduced herself as Jackie and asked me if I wanted music on audio or video. When I said I wanted both, she invited me to sit inside the stall and make selections from numerous music files she had on the computer. She opened the numerous folders and asked me if I wanted any of the songs.

This immediately created a moral dilemma for me. I asked her if there was a store where I could actually purchase original music, and she said there was none. I thought that she was just being a shrewd businesswoman, presenting her music as the only viable option. I decided, once again, to "go native" and purchase her music just like the local people were doing. I convinced myself that while I wanted to support local business by buying original music, this burning of music for sale seemed like a very common occurrence in Kampala. While this is indeed a moral question, we have to acknowledge the reality of low-income levels among potential consumers of this music due to market constraints that limit their disposable income necessary to purchase original music. An original CD of local music would sell for about US$18, and very few consumers can afford it. Without such a market for music on CD, artistes tend to make money through live performances rather than rely on the sale of tapes and CDs. When I attended a performance by Bebe Cool at the Africana Hotel in Kampala in June 2007, I estimated the attendance to be about one thousand people. With each ticket going for at least US$5, it was possible that he made quite some money that night. Music piracy has also created, as Brian Larkin argues for Nigeria, "a legitimate media form that could not exist without the infrastructure created by its illegitimate double, pirate media" (2004, 290). In this way, piracy enables local modes of production and reproduction that make music and other media available to a wider audience.

I made my selections, and Jackie burned them on a blank CD and asked for three thousand Uganda shillings for each. Within an hour, I had more Ugandan music than I could listen to in a day. Was the rest of my research going to be this easy? What did this experience mean? It meant that technological innovations and market constraints had robbed many musicians of their income through pirated music. Yet, it allowed many young people a source of livelihood by selling pirated music, which, in turn, increased the popularity of musicians. It was a Catch-22. Karen Flynn (2005) explores a similar scenario in Mwanza, Tanzania, where she discusses the informal economic activities locally referred to as *biashara ndogo ndogo* (small businesses) that are really not regulated by the government and that allow many people a source of livelihood while denying the government tax revenue. The sale of pirated music at Wandegeya was an illegal operation (at least the stall was), because in the summer 2007 when I was back in Kampala, I found that only bare ground remained where Jackie's music stall once stood. Upon inquiry, I was informed that the city of Kampala was getting ready to clean up its premises especially in readiness for a major commonwealth heads-of-government meeting slated for November 2007 in Kampala.

Not quite convinced that there was no store in Kampala selling original music, I decided to search again. One taxidriver took me to a store that he thought would have local music on CD, but it turned out the store was stocked with American and European music and no local music. I even searched for Ugandan music online at a local Internet café and came across a local address of a company that claimed to have local music for sale. When I called the number supplied, I was told that I needed to give them a day to make the right selection, burn the songs onto a CD, and then deliver it to me. Jackie was right, after all—there were no easily available copies of recorded local music. I went back to Jackie's stall whenever I needed more music, and in the process, she introduced me to Jack, who eventually became my ad hoc local research assistant, mostly transcribing and translating into English a number of songs sung in Luganda.

When I listened to the local music that Jackie had recorded for me, I found out that Bebe Cool's song that I had heard on the radio on my first day in Kampala is titled "Sikiliza (Listen)" and is a collaborative project with another local musician named Yvette. In part of the song, Bebe Cool accuses East African nations of disunity:

> Kenyans do not want to work with Ugandans
> Ugandans do not want to work with Kenyans
> In Zaire people are dying daily, while presidents live so large
> Children sleep hungry while their mothers wail
> There is a big gap between the rich and the poor

East African unity was the subject of great political discussion in June 2007 when Rwanda and Burundi joined the East African Community that had initially included Kenya, Uganda, and Tanzania. The real returns of such unity are variably articulated in terms of economic and political integration, but Bebe Cool's song is quite relevant. In the 2007 national budgets, for instance, the countries' finance ministries tried as much as possible to synchronize taxation and reduce imbalances in trade tariffs. If and when such a community becomes a reality, there will be a much-needed economic and social integration that many hip hop musicians in East Africa have continued to seek. This is the kind of integration and unity that Bebe Cool desires for Africa, even though there are lingering challenges. Kenyan tour operators, for instance, cannot take tourists into Tanzania's national parks using Kenyan vehicles despite both countries sharing national borders and a national park (the Masai Mara on the Kenyan side and the Serengeti on the Tanzanian side). Plans for economic integration through the East African Community will, therefore, have to address such economic realities because member countries have different economic strengths and policies.

While Bebe Cool sees the plight of the poor as a function of disunity and lack of care from the rich and politicians, Uganda's journalist and social critic Andrew Mwenda places the reasons for Africa's poverty on personal desires for self-aggrandizement. He also sees Africa's political challenges tied to its agrarian economy that was abruptly changed into a colonially inspired structure: "[O]ur democratic process in Uganda has been crippled by bread and butter issues: Members of Parliament are bribed to change political positions for as little as Shs. 5m [US$3,000]. Imagine! Some trade values in exchange for a ministerial job. And what is the ultimate aim? To drive a good car and live in a good house. The price: destroying any possibility of sustaining progressive change in our countries and therefore the future of our children" (2006, 7). This politicoeconomic reality expressed here by Mwenda attends in Kenya and Tanzania as well as in many other African countries. Stories abound, for instance, of governments in Africa where their representatives collude with unscrupulous Western companies to dump toxic waste in African land for a small bribe.[8] As Bebe Cool notes above, the gap between the poor and the rich is big in Africa. Many of the poor can hardly meet their basic needs while the rich continue to amass wealth.

The next section analyzes the critiques leveled by hip hop artistes against governments that are unable to respond positively to this material gap, especially within the context of a neoliberal agenda for privatized social-service delivery. Issues presented by these artistes reveal a crisis of governance and the crippling of the economy especially as the role of government as a social-service provider has been greatly reduced by market-based economic models.

Consequently, privatization, employment and retrenchment, and health-care provision are issues high on the discursive terrain of these artistes and the constituencies they represent.

Privatization, Investment, and Increased Marginality

As a policy for economic change in Africa, privatization represents a radical departure from the previous arrangement where the government was the central player in public policy. As argued especially in chapter 2, the government in East Africa took up the role of bringing socioeconomic and political change soon after independence. The initial plan was to have a centralized government that would right the wrongs done by European colonialism, including an attempt to distribute the national cake equitably to all citizens (Nyerere 1968). Indeed, the first three presidents of the three East African countries saw the role of their governments as that of reorienting the wheel of development from the one set by colonialism, which had been guided by narrow economic self-interest to benefit Europeans, to one that benefited their respective citizens by providing education opportunities, health care, and meaningful economic activities. A number of programs were adopted by these presidents to address the economic challenges facing their young nations soon after independence.

In 1967, for instance, Julius Nyerere, president of Tanzania, issued the famous Arusha Declaration, which urged his counterparts in Africa to withdraw from the world's economic system dominated by the West (Nyang'oro 2002). He advocated a policy of self-reliance (*kujitegemea*) instead of adhering to the Western economic models of international trade, aid, and private investment (Nyerere 1968). However, very few, if any, governments could build alternative economic systems outside global systems already entrenched through colonialism and Westernization (Crowder 1987b; Mamdani 1996; Throup and Hornsby 1998; Throup 1993; Widner 1992). They had to follow the existing global economic structures while trying to adequately address their local challenges. Many African governments expanded their participation and control of national investment through import substitution, industrialization, and marketing boards for cash crops such as tea, coffee, cotton, and pyrethrum. They also used other measures such as price controls on producer and consumer goods, fixed interest and exchange rates, and ownership and management of state and parastatal enterprises such as postal services, electricity, water, insurance, and banks (Ajayi 2001; Mkandawire 2002). This allowed the governments to have a firm grip on the economy while also acting as the largest employer (Bayart 1993). In the 1980s, for instance, there was so much control on foreign currency that travelers going abroad from East Africa had to record in their passports the amount of foreign exchange they carried out of the country. As recently as 1992, for instance, I had the specific amount of "student allowance" in U.S. dollars entered into the last page on my passport and endorsed by a bank when I left Kenya for further studies in the United States. Later, in the mid-1990s, this rule was discarded when liberalization and privatization became the new modes of operation (Chabal 2002).

As foreign debt overwhelmed many governments, structural adjustment programs (SAPs) kicked in and paved way for privatization as the mandated economic policy for East Africa and beyond. This new strategy left East African governments weak and unable to provide the services they had provided soon after independence. The majority of the population that depended on the government for jobs and social services felt abandoned and condemned to a life of misery. How can one explain to a poor mother why she needs to pay for medical services at the local health center when such a service was given free and when she can hardly afford the minimum charge, anyway? Maybe we can tell her that this is a result of a public policy called privatization, in which the role of the government as a manager of social services has been taken up by private enterprise. Such a reality has not eluded the keen eye of many hip hop artistes. As Wagosi wa Kaya show in their song "Tumeshtuka (We are shocked)," something of a mystery surrounds privatization:

> What do we gain through privatization?
> What do we gain through privatization, we are in shock
> We got independence in 1961 yet today our [economic] development
>   is stunted
> Where are we headed, my fellow Tanzanians?
> It seems as if we are not aware of where we are
> We have been told a lot about privatization yet nothing makes sense

The Swahili term used by Wagosi wa Kaya in this song in reference to what I have translated as privatization is *ubia*. This is a word that can also refer to partnerships that come with privatization as local investors team up with foreigners to buy parastatal and government enterprises. As Wagosi wa Kaya state, the majority of population have no clue as to how this privatization project works. The measures taken by East African governments to implement the privatization models of economic policies were not well explained to the local people that the policies would adversely affect. In an attempt to explain what privatization means, Wagosi wa Kaya link it to European takeover of local industries and natural resources:

> The Europeans are not for us don't be deceived
> The ports, mines, and everything else [they have taken over]
> While the citizens live like orphans
> The Europeans talk to us in distractions
> The things they do unto us you would think we are blind
> We are tricked to embrace this privatization
> Yet if you scrutinize carefully, you will see that we are being ripped off
> Wake up, fellow Tanzanians
> Make haste, the Europeans are ripping us off

Many projects reflect this reality that Wagosi wa Kaya talk about in this song. Many companies and social-service providers in East Africa are now owned by private investors, making their services almost unattainable by the poor. Access to health-care services even in small rural clinics requires user fees, and water and electricity entail payments to establish service and for the subsequent consumer charges. This has placed a heavy economic burden on many individuals, families, and communities. A report by Kenya's daily newspaper the *Daily Nation,* for instance, shows the economic burdens placed on individuals that result in many HIV/AIDS patients selling their antiretroviral drugs in order to purchase food (Ngesa 2007). Such dire strategies can be linked directly to the collapse of the economy as the nation-state retreats due to SAPs and other forms of neoliberal economic programs. Wagosi wa Kaya continue with their commentary on this economic restructuring:

> Your majesty, king of privatization
> What is it that you want from our country?
> When a guest visits a home, (s)he is welcomed into the lounge
> But the government has allowed her/him into the bedroom
> This guest I am talking about is privatization
> It has taken over all the major corporations
> Not quite satisfied, it has gone on to take over even the mines

The use of the metaphor of a house and how far a guest is allowed in symbolizes the perception of the breakdown of control over public economic and political structures. The local people have even lost control of their own lives as represented by the invasion of their privacy as the guest (privatization) takes over their private space and enters the bedroom. In many communities in East Africa, guests are never allowed to enter any other space in the house except the lounge or living room. The bedroom is reserved for family members or relatives and very close friends. That privatization has transcended this cultural restriction reveals a feeling of disenfranchisement among many East Africans who can hardly make ends meet. This loss of control seems to be best exemplified by the loss of gainful employment through retrenchment and poor health services, again exacerbated by neoliberal economic programs.

Retrenchment and Other Economic Blues

Part of the structural changes required by the SAPs instituted by the World Bank and IMF include reduction of people employed in the civil-service sector (Strange 1996). Governments were asked to reduce their employees through the process of retrenchment as a way to cut their total fiscal expenditures (Biersteker 1990). In the process, many civil servants were laid off, adding to the already high number of the unemployed. There is no question that the provision of services in the public sector has been glaringly inefficient in East Africa with many public/civil servants abetting and perpetuating corruption (Ferguson 2006). Yet, one cannot assume that privatizing such services is the panacea for efficiency because what is considered a "bloated civil service" has provided a livelihood for thousands, if not millions, of East Africans (Amin 1998; Mkandawire and Soludo 1999). With struggling economies that cannot truly support expansive private business and investment, government employment has been the backbone of East Africa's public service.

As noted above, postindependence East African governments, especially in the 1960s, used their booming export revenues to finance the expansion of free health and education for their newly enfranchised citizens. By the end of the 1990s, Kenya's civil service, for instance, accounted for 40 percent of government's recurrent expenditure. By 1997, Tanzania, Uganda, and Kenya had retrenched 30 percent, 40 percent, and 10 percent of their civil servants, respectively (Mutahaba and Kiragu 2002, 34). This downsizing seemed like the best strategy to reduce public spending as measures supported by the World Bank and IMF's Public (Civil) Service Reform and Management (PRSM) were considered the best in accomplishing such a feat. This reality is not lost to hip hop artistes, who have to grapple with the lack of political power to reverse this while also struggling to understand the process itself. Wagosi wa Kaya address the issue of retrenchment in their song "Vinatia Uchungu (It's painful)" and show the unexplained rationale for it:

> When you see people declared redundant [laid off], don't assume that
> they were lazy
> That is just the reality in Tanzania today . . .
> This is too much, how can I just lose my job?
> If it is education, I have been up to Makerere [University]
> The same place that Nyerere went; I was not hired on forged certificates

The process of retrenchment is a shocker for many, especially those who assume that job security is attained through qualifications and the right kind of education or credentials. Yet, under the PSRM, it's not about qualifications as it is about reducing government's recurrent expenditure. Despite massive retrenchment undertaken by governments in East Africa, it is now becoming clear that reducing civil-service jobs does not always produce the desired results. In a report on retrenchment (downsizing), George Yambesi concludes that retrenchment had little link to improvement in service delivery and that salaries remained low despite the initial promise of efficiency and improvement of terms of service in the civil service (2004). Not all people in East Africa were regularly affected by SAPs and other programs pushed by the IMF and World Bank under neoliberalism. Local elites, for instance, benefited from the failure of the state as they cashed in on cheap imports and were also employed and involved in civil society following the proliferation of nongovernmental organizations (NGOs). In some cases, the so-called bloated civil service did not meet the demands of the population because certain sectors of the civil service did not have enough workers to meet the needs of the population. This may explain why, in June 2007, the Kenyan government had decided to hire an additional eleven thousand teachers to meet the demand for teachers in the country following increased enrolment after free primary education was implemented in 2003. How can retrenchment work for the good of such nations if they need to meet real demands of their citizens? It cannot work, because the proponents of such programs forget, as Chinua Achebe has said, that "Africa is people" (1998) and not just statistics. Angered by the lack of empathy towards Africa as Western technocrats praised SAPs, Achebe told a gathering of European and American bankers and economists,

> Here you are, spinning your fine theories to be tried out in your imaginary
> laboratories. You are developing new drugs and feeding them to a bunch of
> laboratory guinea pigs and hoping for the best. I have news for you. Africa is
> not fiction. Africa is people, real people. Have you thought of that? You are

brilliant people, world experts. You may even have the very best intentions. But have you thought, really thought, of Africa as people? I will tell you the experience of my own country, Nigeria, with structural adjustment. After two years of this remedy we saw the country's minimum wage fall in value from the equivalent of 15 British pounds to 5 pounds a month. This is not a lab report; it is not a mathematical exercise. We are talking about someone whose income, which is already miserable enough, is now reduced to one-third of what it was two years ago. And this flesh-and-blood man has a wife and children. You say he should simply go home and tell them to be patient. Now let me ask you this question. Would you recommend a similar remedy to your own government? (1998, 9)

Western technocrats are willing to recommend economic structures to Africa in doses and measures that they are unwilling to recommend to their own nations. When these structures are added to an already impoverished community, numerous problems engulf the people. Some of these problems include poor health and vulnerability to HIV/AIDS. These and hip hop responses to these problems are the subjects of the next chapter.

5

Morality, Health, and the Politics of Sexuality in an Era of HIV/AIDS

Many of you despise AIDS patients
You laugh at me, why don't you go get tested?
If you really care, go to the testing center
Save your children by declaring your status

—Professor Jay, "Msinitenge (Don't abandon me)"

Music and Sexuality in the Context of HIV/AIDS

In July 2004, Kenya's hip hop artistes Circute and Jo-el were traveling to Nakuru (a town west of Nairobi) for a live performance. Before their trip commenced, the public transportation they were traveling in was taken to Nairobi's Central Police Station for a security check. The artistes were traveling at a time when carjacking was rampant in Kenya, and thugs often masqueraded as passengers, and when the bus or whatever vehicle they were in got to a "convenient" place, the thugs would hijack a vehicle at gunpoint and rob passengers of all their valuables. To deal with this menace, most long-distance public service vehicles were driven into a police station, and all passengers checked for any weapons. Once at the police station, the practice was for all passengers to get out of the vehicle and have police officers perform a bodycheck for any weapons. The vehicle carrying Circute and Jo-el got to the police station, and the officer on duty went on to conduct a regular check on all passengers. When the officer found eight hundred condoms in Circute's jacket and many in Jo-el's travel bag, he seemed irritated and asked them in Kiswahili, "*Kwani hizi condoms zote mnapeleka wapi* (where are you taking all these condoms)?" Circute explained to the officer that he was carrying condoms to distribute to their fans in Nakuru as they had done in the past and that they were trying to live up to their song "Juala" (local slang for plastic bag), which urges people to use condoms. The song, produced in 2004, became both popular and controversial. It warns people against unprotected sex and refers to women as *manyake* (slang for meat). On recognizing who they were, a female passenger in the same vehicle said to the duo, "So you are the *manyakes*. Shame on you! You have belittled girls and women, describing them as sex objects. Your song is really stupid."[1]

This telling story opens us up to an interesting discussion of social matters that are often left out of public discourse. The reaction of the police officer to Circute and Jo-el carrying condoms and the chiding they received for their lyrics both point to the complexity surrounding matters related to sex and sexuality. This chapter discuss this complexity by using hip hop music as a window to interrogate and understand the silence surrounding sex and sexuality in East Africa in an era of HIV/AIDS. A selection of hip hop artistes whose songs allow for an intersection between hip hop, gender, and sexuality in East Africa's public space are highlighted, and argue that hip hop is a new medium that, if used appropriately, will slowly engage the youth in public discourse on sexuality. When such a medium is mobilized appropriately, it can lead to a reconstitution of discursive responses to the HIV/AIDS pandemic and join many other organizations that have also used other media forms to sensitize the public on many social and cultural issues. These include, for instance, radio programs on sexuality spearheaded by Twaweza Communications in Kenya, television programs on civic engagement, sexuality, and reproductive health in Tanzania through Femina Health Information Project and by Uganda's Straight Talk Foundation that has been central in health and development communication especially for youth.[2]

Following Victor Turner's notion of social dramas and their role in creating frames that go beyond the everyday (1974), I present hip hop as a frame that allows for a discussion of that which is often hidden from the public. The responses that Circute and Jo-el received were not an isolated incident; there have been numerous criticisms raised against their song. The duo had engaged in what is often considered a taboo topic for public mention and discussion. One of the verses in the song asks people to "use protection to avoid diseases and infections" because "African men are obsessed with sex." The song goes on to ask, "Do you have condoms, or will you end up facing the mortuary ceiling like a fool?" It is clear that the song has an important message for society regarding sex in the context of HIV/AIDS. However, the irritating thing about the song for many is the reference made to women as *manyake*, which is a word derived from the slang word *nyake* used by youth to refer to meat instead of the Kiswahili word *nyama* (meat). The prefix *ma-* in *manyake* is a plural form marker that is quite commonly used in Kiswahili and other Bantu languages. The female passenger was right that the song belittles women by referring to them as meat. Interestingly, the use of the concept of meat in reference to women is not new in Kenya's popular music. The group Them Mushrooms recorded a song titled "Nyambura" (a person's name) that became quite popular in the 1990s. The song talks about how much the man loves his female friend. He says that he loves her as much as he loves grilled meat (see Ntarangwi 1999, for further discussion of this song).

In defense of their song and lyrics, Circute and Jo-el say, "The people who are yelling that the song is filthy have not even listened to the message that is carried in the song. The reason why people are complaining is because of the word 'Manyake' and they think it is dirty. We are not degrading women, what are they made of? Flesh, which is meat! Kenyans should stop being hypocrites. They know that these things happen but they want to be confined to their bedroom walls and in darkness, without caring about the consequences. It is true that people are having their fun and we all know it. Let them use protection."[3]

Condoms, Morality, and the Culture of Silence

That a hip hop song talks publicly about sex and the use of condoms is quite bold in East Africa, where there is a lot of secrecy around such matters. It is especially interesting that as they defended their lyrics in the interview cited above, they are unable to use the same language they have used in the song. They, for instance, do not mention sex in the above conversation and only use indirect phrases such as "these things happen" and "having their fun." This is because the culture of silence that surrounds sex and sexuality in many East African communities is very much linked to language use and its attendant contexts. Even though majority of East Africans are sexually active, there is no public discourse on sex and sexuality even as HIV/AIDS continues to claim many lives each day. To discuss sex or even mention it in public is to not only cross certain moral boundaries but also draw the ire of the public, often bringing upon oneself some level of condemnation. The shock and irritation expressed by the police officer when checking Circute and Jo-el as well as the castigation they received from a female passenger all attest to this unspoken moral code as well as culture of silence and the disdain attached to it. While the use of the word *manyake* in reference to women is offensive, my argument here is that the mere mention of sex and use of condoms in a song meant for public consumption was in itself the cause of much of the negative feedback Circute and Jo-el received from the public. That the artistes were themselves unable to talk about sex openly in their interview testifies to the power of music in traversing social terrains that are often considered unutterable in public. As I have argued elsewhere, "Music has been an important forum that has been used to mediate social issues in ways that many other fora that are used for dispensing public information, have been unable to exhaustively accomplish" (2005, 303).

Music will continue to be important because the public discussion of sex and sexuality has been a tough project for many communities in East Africa, especially as they respond to the threat of HIV/AIDS. Other than Uganda, which took a very proactive stance on sex and sexuality in public through its ABC (abstinence, be faith, use condoms) program, both Kenya and Tanzania have been very slow at embracing a similar stance. Indeed, even in Uganda, the message about abstinence and condom use was presented in a context in which there really was no discussion of the pleasures and attractions of sexual activity that would lead one to be infected with the disease (Parikh 2005, 125). The ABC program introduced sex in public discourse but only in a sanitized way that did not have any real discussion of sex. A number of factors can explain this avoidance of public discourse on sex and sexuality. Talking about sex in public hinges on notions of morality, and churches play a key role in defining and regulating it. Due to the links often made among HIV/AIDS, sex, condom use, and promiscuity, promoting condoms as a way to reduce HIV/AIDS infections has received heavy opposition from many churches in East Africa.

A report titled "This We Teach and Do" by the Secretariat Commission of the Catholic church in Kenya reiterates the Church's stance against the promotion of condoms as a way to fight HIV/AIDS infection and instead advocates for abstinence and going back to "traditional African practices that rewarded virgin-brides." In Tanzania, the scenario is quite similar. In 2005, the *East African*, a weekly newspaper distributed in East Africa, reported that Bishop Kilaini, assistant to the head of the Catholic Church in Tanzania, argued that condoms were not the answer to the HIV/AIDS scourge. Bishop Kilaini said, according to the article, "Condoms are used only for fornication, which is going against God's commandments. Those advocating the use of condoms are selfish men who want the Church to bless them while they break the sixth Commandment. The Church cannot encourage immorality and promiscuity; condoms have been there even before the AIDS scourge hit the world."[4]

Promotion, especially in public, of condom use has been regarded as a gateway to immoral behavior, and the Catholic Church has been very vocal against campaigns for condom use. This blanket condemnation of condom use ignores cases of discordant couples where one spouse is HIV/AIDS positive, and the other is negative.[5] Recognizing this reality, Bishop Benjamin Nzimbi of the Anglican Church in Kenya has asked "discordant couples to use condoms."[6] This softened stance on condom use, even though an exception, is important because of the influence the Anglican Church has on the East African population, especially in such institutions as education. East African governments and others committed to reversing the tide of HIV/AIDS pandemic cannot, however, ignore the churches when they oppose campaigns for condom use. The Catholic Church, for instance, is very prominent in East Africa; it supports many schools where respective governments have yet to have a consensus on the teaching of sex education in all schools. If the Catholic Church's stand is to oppose condom use and maintain that condom use will not be part of sex education in schools, then most people will likely adhere to that stand. A proposal to introduce sex education in Tanzania, for instance, had to be shelved following strong opposition from the country's followers of the Islamic faith as well as the Catholic Church.[7] In Uganda, the Catholic Church continues to be opposed to the use of condoms, prompting President Yoweri Museveni to ask the Church to drop its opposition and support condom use as a way of fighting HIV/AIDS infections.[8] Opposition to condoms especially from the Catholic Church and the promotion of abstinence can also be tied to U.S. pressure, especially under President George W. Bush, who, through neoconservative ideology, has linked foreign aid to abstinence and opposition to condoms especially under the President's Emergency Plan for AIDS Relief (PEPFAR) program (see www.pepfar.org).

The condom is an important symbol for understanding the dynamics of sex and sexuality in East Africa. Opposition to condom use also ties closely to the mystery that surrounds sex and sexuality, especially in Christian households. Njeri Mbugua's research shows that many children raised in Christian homes are more likely than their non-Christian counterparts to have very little, if any, sex education at home, because talking about sex is considered "dirty" language and unchristian (Mbugua 2007). Mbugua attributes this to a Christian moral ethic instilled by "European missionaries [who] discouraged the use of 'dirty' language that was used when the extended members of the family gave sex education to the young" (2007, 1081).

On the whole, therefore, discourse on sex and the Catholic Church and its stand on morality, which, in turn, tends to trickle down to the youth, who then grow up with a very specific ideology about sex and sexuality, increasingly shapes sexuality. Lucy Kangara shares some responses she received from a study on Christian youth and sexuality in rural Kenya in which she shows that a number of boys still expect women to be ignorant and quiet about sex and sexuality. One respondent, Kangara says, "a boy from [a] Church commented that 'if a girl starts a topic about "those things" I will definitely know she is loose and I will try to avoid her'" (2005, 9). What this boy is reproducing is a discourse that normalizes male knowledge about sex and sexuality while demonizing that of the female. Such claims and wishes, even among youth in church, half of whom in 1998 were estimated to be sexually active, have to be assessed in light of increased sexuality (Achieng 1998). Consequently, as some want to maintain a culture of female ignorance about sex and sexuality, the reality is that many are already sexually active and need the knowledge even more. In further findings, Kangara gives a following observation that further reveals this increased "Victorian" attitude towards sex and sexuality among some youth: "None of the respondents mentioned church leaders or their parents as being the source of information about sexuality issues. Relationships between boys and girls are highly censored, as they are labeled 'immoral.' On whether they embrace sexuality discussion within the Church a female respondent said [it does] 'as long as it is conducted outside our church because we will be a bit free to ask some questions'" (2005, 20).

This "don't ask, don't tell" attitude towards sexuality in church as shown by both Kangara (2005) and Mbugua (2007) may not be a reflection of sexual reality in the respective communities. Otherwise, how do we explain the high numbers of HIV/AIDS infection rates in East Africa where Christians constitute up to 70 percent of the total population? It appears that Christians may profess a faith that dictates a certain lifestyle that would enable them manage and control the threat of HIV/AIDS but then still engage in the affairs of the "world," probably because sexuality issues are seen and understood as largely private activities that are subject to varying degrees of social, cultural, religious, moral, and legal norms. The question that lingers is that of how best to approach sexuality as communities struggle with HIV/AIDS.

Organizations such as Family Health International (FHI) and World Health Organization (WHO) have argued that providing women with a female condom or a microbicide is an example of a strategy that can enhance women's real power. A woman's power to say no or yes to sex is important in controlling not only her sexuality but also in protecting her from sexually transmitted diseases or unplanned pregnancies. The high rates of HIV/AIDS infections among women in East Africa do reflect the power imbalances that exist between men and women. Providing women with condoms recognizes that condoms are an axis of personal power and intimately tied to social power.

The male condom, for instance, is technology that men control, using it at will and having control over both their own sexuality and that of their female partners (G. R. Gupta 2000). A study conducted in Tanzania (Maman, Mbwambo, Hogan, Kilonzo, and Sweat [1999]) found that there were gender differences in the decision-making process involving men and women when seeking the now-growing free HIV Voluntary Counseling and Testing (VCT) services. While men made independent decisions to seek voluntary counseling and testing, women felt compelled to discuss their own testing with their partners before accessing the service, the study concluded. This arrangement creates a potential barrier to accessing VCT services by women because when they disclose their intent to visit the centers, their male partners tend to dissuade them from doing so and in the process create unnecessary tensions and mistrust as the women are often blamed and accused of infidelity. Women have, therefore, to negotiate their relationships with men as they make such individual decisions about their sexual behavior.

Condom use by women would take into account this imbalance of power in sexual interaction that, in turn, makes it difficult for women to negotiate whether to use a condom with their male partners. By providing women with an alternate, woman-initiated technology, they will be able to control a number of sexual practices in their lives. Although all this is laudable, we must be cautious when recommending condoms for women because of the prevailing power imbalances. If women have to negotiate with their partners their intentions to visit a VCT center, then using a condom with those partners might prove problematic. Moreover, women's access to condoms is especially undermined by their lack of economic power and independence. Access to power for women has, therefore, to be grounded in tangible socioeconomic changes that will benefit women directly. The more women become economically independent, the more they will be able to access individual power necessary in making decisions about their sexuality and sex lives. This is because even men, who tend to have more economic power than women, may not always afford or have access to condoms as they wish (Nzioka 2004), and at times when condoms are available, they may be considered contraceptive tools rather than protection against infections (Wakabi 2006), calling for a multifaceted approach to issues of sex and sexuality.

The Condom as a Signifier of Discourse on Sexuality

The realities of power, choice, and condoms addressed here may seem quite daunting in the face of HIV/AIDS. Is the Catholic Church justified in its opposition to condoms? People continue to die even as awareness and access to condoms are rising. Is the condom a useless resource in countering the spread of HIV/AIDS? The condom is important in the fight against HIV/AIDS specifically because it has become a signifier and a platform for public discourse on sex and sexuality in East Africa. Irrespective of how we consider the condom in society, be it in its use in sexual union, one's ability to acquire and use it, or when and how to use it, all these boil down to its symbolic role of engaging East Africans in public discussion of sex and sexuality. The condom has slowly turned into a window through which to enter into East Africa's private domain of sex and sexuality, allowing a glimpse into people's perceptions, attitudes, and knowledge about sex and sexuality. What people say about the condom, how they relate with its sale and use, and when and where it can be discussed all point to deeper issues of morality and how they are perceived both in private and public.

An example is a Kenya condom advertisement that depicts a busy street in downtown Nairobi with many pedestrians and cars present. A police officer directs traffic, and many people cross the streets. At the center of the advertisement are a young woman and a young man walking in opposite directions until their eyes meet. It has just stopped raining, and the young woman decides to close and store her umbrella. She tries to put the umbrella in its cover but the cover is blown away by the wind. The young man walks to her, places his bag down, and pulls out a condom from his pocket and then tears it open. The crowd stops, and the police officer directing traffic stops as the camera focuses on the crowd watching the young man and woman. The man proceeds to slowly put the condom over the woman's umbrella to replace the cover that was blown away. As he finishes, the stupefied crowd cheers and celebrates, and the camera focuses on a couple in a private vehicle where an older man is laughing and cheering much to his female partner's dislike. At the bottom of the screen come the slogan *"Maisha iko sawa na Trust"* (life is fine with Trust). Trust is a brand of condom widely sold in Kenya. This advertisement presents an interesting and bold way to insert sex and sexuality into the public sphere. The condom has allowed people to publicly talk about sex and sexuality in unprecedented ways.

As traditional institutions charged with sex education continue to diminish, and secrecy becomes a facet that surrounds sex education in formal schools, many young people, especially girls, will continually be unable to ask for information about sex out of fear that they will be thought of as sexually active and loose. This is the secrecy that is being challenged through popular culture, especially hip hop music and dance that introduce bold ways of public presentation of sex and sexuality. This presentation has not been warmly received. Many hip hop songs and their performances may be deemed unacceptable and at times "un-African," as Circute and Jo-el's song "Juala" did, yet they help open up spaces for public discourse on sex and sexuality. In so doing they allow youth to have various opportunities through which to change the prevailing culture of silence in the face of HIV/AIDS pandemic.

Hip Hop and Silence on Sex and Sexuality

One way to deal with the culture of silence around sex and sexuality is to encourage social attitudes and practices that do not conform to traditional expectations of masculinity and femininity. This is a facet that a number of hip hop musicians have already engaged with and caused some social tensions in their various communities and across the region as they have confronted harsh criticism. This boldness of presenting controversial material is in part due to the complex role music plays in society in general (Ogude 2007). Music is a platform that allows for unprecedented ways of talking about taboo topics. Circute and Jo-el's song "Juala" and the response they got from a female passenger when they were found with condoms in their pockets offer some useful examples of music as a new platform through which to navigate public discourse on sexuality. This change is not limited to music, because weekly popular newspapers have started to emerge as other venues through which to engage similar discourse.

In June 2007, for instance, Tanzania's popular Swahili weekly magazine *Nipashe* (inform me) ran numerous stories of men and women caught cheating on their spouses in which were included pictures of the "culprits," many of them naked. I spoke with one newspaper vendor in Dar es Salaam regarding these weekly reports, and he mentioned that this was becoming a common occurrence. I quickly learned of other stories, some involving schoolteachers and other public leaders. This was almost unheard of a few years earlier when there were fewer newspapers, radio stations, and other public media, all of which were at the time regulated by the government. Currently, it seems as if the liberalization of media has ushered in a new culture of public information. A story published in an April 2007 issue of *Nipashe* reported that villagers and students from Bukoli Secondary School in Geita District, Tanzania, beat up a teacher who allegedly had sex with a female student (Masuguliko 2007). While *Nipashe* and other similar newspapers may be considered "tabloids" in Tanzania, they play the role of highlighting some of the social issues of the day and consequently opening up public discourse on sexuality. These "tabloids" together with hip hop music are important avenues through which the public engages with matters of sexuality that have hitherto been private.

As these media create platforms for having some discourse on sex and sexuality, there is also an urgent need to focus on the imbalance of power between men and women in matters of sex and sexuality. It is clear now that women are more negatively affected by HIV/AIDS than men. Statistics released at the eighth Triennial Commonwealth Women's Affairs Ministers meeting, "Financing Gender Equality for Development and Democracy," held in Kampala, Uganda from June 11 to 14, 2007, show that women and girls in British Commonwealth countries make up a third of all HIV infections,[9] and women between fifteen and twenty-four years old in sub-Saharan Africa are twice more likely to be infected with the virus than men of the same age.[10] Recent statistics place the rate of HIV/AIDS in Uganda, Kenya, and Tanzania at 6.7 percent, 6.1 percent, and 6.5 percent, respectively (UNAIDS 2006). What is alarming is that Uganda's rate of infection is going up despite the great strides made in the 1990s. A study by Leigh Shafer (2006) in both urban and rural Uganda shows some communities with HIV/AIDS rates of up to 8.9 percent for women and 5.7 percent for men.

This gendered reality of HIV/AIDS can be linked to prevailing cultural norms and expectations including unequal power relations and different sociocultural expectations on sexuality for both men and women. There is, for instance, an unspoken cultural expectation for "good-mannered" women to be ignorant about sex and passive in sexual interactions. For men, it is expected that they will be well trained in sexual acts and will usually take the lead in any sexual encounter. The lack of knowledge on sex and sexuality increases women's risk of infection and places great demands on male virility. Any woman who talks about or desires sex publicly or displays knowledge of sex is considered loose and not fit for marriage. Many women are unaware of many issues relating to their own sexuality and often find it difficult to negotiate for safer sex even with consistent partners. Men who are not familiar with sexual acts or are virgins are themselves effeminized or considered abnormal. Geeta R. Gupta argues, "[M]en in many societies are socialized to be self-reliant, not to show their emotions, and not to seek assistance in times of need or stress. This expectation of invulnerability associated with being a man runs counter to the expectation that men should protect themselves from potential infection and encourages the denial of risk" (2000, 3).

Various ways and strategies can and have been taken to respond to all these challenges pertaining to sex and sexuality in East Africa. One level to consider here is the way in which masculine and feminine identities are constructed, mobilized, and maintained in much of East Africa, and both popular and traditional music have contributed to that process. A number of hip hop artistes have composed and continue to perform songs that critique or reconstitute received notions of gender identities and in the process offer important scenarios of responding to the challenges of sex and sexuality. Uganda's Jose Chameleone's "Mama Mia" is a good example of a song that encourages social attitudes and practices that may not conform to traditional expectations of gender. In the song, Chameleone presents a case of "positive deviance," where a man is constructed in gender-equitable attitudes that reconstitute masculine identities. Narrating a man's tribulations following the departure of his wife, "Mama Mia" provides a story of a woman who leaves her husband after they have had eight children together. Playing the role of the "dumped" man, Chameleone asks why the wife left him, leaving him with the children who are at home crying; why she dumped him, making him cry, because even men cry. This message is repeated throughout the song as the singer gives various reasons why he, as the husband, is the most suitable lover and partner.

As stated in chapter 4, it is unusual for men to publicly admit that they are crying, especially over a woman or after being dumped by a woman. It is against the received cultural norm in many East African communities for men to cry because part of masculine identity is built around men's ability to withstand all life's challenges without shedding a tear. By introducing a "softer side" of masculine identity, Chameleone is attempting to encourage a different reading of gendered behavior, one that acknowledges men's emotional attributes. It is also a more nuanced way of looking at received and actual social attitudes and practices around masculine and feminine identities. Men may not want to admit that they cry in public, but in reality, they do cry and project their "weaker" side even if it is done outside of public view. Breaking through the web of received/traditional masculine identity would allow for both men and women to plough through the expectations of sexuality that are covered in secrecy and silence and in the process also breakdown the veneer that shields social relations from public scrutiny.

Tanzania's Mr. Ebbo presents another example of gender identity but from a slightly different angel on masculine "power." He argues that although many people (especially men) may consider women the "weaker sex," women are in reality stronger and wield a lot of power over men. In his song "Muwe na Huruma (Be merciful)," Mr. Ebbo says:

Friends say that women are weak and should not be allowed
    to make decisions
How can you not see that women have control of this world?
If the woman is weak, how come when she asks for five
    hundred shillings
You get confused and give her a thousand?
And don't say it's love because when your siblings ask for money
You never give them a cent!

Mr. Ebbo adopts an interesting analysis of social relations that transcends the normal presentation of women as weak and men as strong. He almost adopts a "weapons of the weak" (Scott 1985) approach in which the seemingly weak tend to have access to power that is often outside of that which is publicly sanctioned or accepted. In the song "Muwe na Huruma," Mr. Ebbo shows that women have a grip on men in a way that is outside of the usual public realm and as a result projects women to be much stronger than received wisdom may accord them. This kind of power, however, needs to be mobilized to make concrete social changes. It is not enough for women to have "hidden" power; they need power that is publicly acknowledged and one that is accessible to all women irrespective of their social status. What Chameleone and Mr. Ebbo have done is challenge the prevailing discourse on gender identities by clearly indicating that social relations between men and women are more complex than many may project or even portend. This way of seeing gender identity and power can be extended to matters of sexuality in the context of HIV/AIDS.

Hip Hop and Responses to HIV/AIDS

The period between 2000 and 2007 witnessed an increased presence of hip hop songs that address issues pertaining to HIV/AIDS in East Africa. Many of those songs address basic issues of HIV/AIDS, such as modes of transmission of the virus, social behavior that may boost or minimize infection, and the way people living with AIDS are perceived and treated by the public and relatives. A number of hip hop songs about HIV/AIDS are composed by artistes out of their own desire to make a difference in the high rate of infection or in response to a request by a private or public organization directly dealing with the pandemic. In this latter case, the organization pays the musicians for the project. Irrespective of the catalyst for composing such songs, it is clear that hip hop has become an important medium through which to communicate with and reach the youth. This is important because the youth is the group most affected by HIV/AIDS.

There are two major categories of hip hop songs on HIV/AIDS. The first category includes songs that burst the bubble of silence that surrounds sex and sexuality. These are songs that talk openly about sex and sexuality and may often be considered as stepping outside of what is socially acceptable in moral decorum. Circute and Jo-el's song "Juala" fits into this category. The second category includes songs that reflect the prevailing status and attitude towards public campaigns for HIV/AIDS. Here are songs that center around dissemination of information about HIV/AIDS—its causes, ways to avoid infection, and relations with those already infected. Songs such as Wagosi wa Kaya's "Titamtambuaje (How do we recognize him/her)" and Professor Jay's "Msinitenge (Don't abandon me)," discussed below, fall under this category. Further, there are songs that tend to combine both categories while others stand on their own.

Wagosi wa Kaya's song "Titamtambuaje" deals with a number of issues related to HIV/AIDS and starts by expressing the challenge faced by communities as they confront the AIDS scourge. The song makes a general observation on the threat of the disease:

> This is a great misfortune, my friends
> Many of us have lost both parents since AIDS spread in this world
> It kills the rich and poor alike
> If you joke around, you will end up in the grave

The song's title "Titamtambuaje" that in this context translates to "How do we recognize someone with HIV/AIDS?" fits into the earlier realm of HIV/AIDS campaigns that were geared towards disseminating information about the disease and how it can be spread. Many people thought that they could recognize a person carrying the virus by simply observing the person's physical state. In a region where there are many people who still die of curable and preventable diseases such as malaria, tuberculosis, diarrhea and meningitis, knowing the symptoms of a disease is an important step towards positive health-seeking behavior. In the case of HIV/AIDS, however, this poses a major challenge because someone may carry the virus and yet fail to have any physical manifestations of it. This may be hard to fathom in communities that are used to dealing with very clear presentations of disease. In many African cultures, the concept of living with a disease is unfathomable and may explain why some people with a disease such as diabetes are known to seek the help of traditional healers who promise them complete cure. HIV/

AIDS may present similar challenges if one is seeking complete cure. In the event that this does not happen, people may resort to other crude methods, including ones such as those reported in Southern Africa where men believe they can get cured of HIV/AIDS if they have sex with virgins (Ahmad 2001). The question that emerges then is how to give public information on HIV/AIDS in order to produce the best results.

When they state in their song "Titamtambuaje" that anyone can contract HIV/AIDS, Wagosi wa Kaya might be considered outdated because this is information that many people now know. However, despite the seemingly explosion of information on HIV/AIDS, there is still a number of new infections each year. This may explain Wagosi wa Kaya's frustration:

> Men and women, let us ask ourselves, how will the AIDS scourge end?
> Every day there are announcements on radio
> On the road there are numerous billboards . . .
> Yet all this advice enters into one ear and out the other

In the 1980s and early 1990s, numerous resources were put towards the dissemination of information regarding HIV/AIDS. Educating the public and creating an AIDS awareness was the key focus of the time. Yet, as Wagosi wa Kaya show in this song, this did not lead to the desired behavior change as information "entered into one ear and went out the other." Many people are aware of the threat of HIV/AIDS, but there is not enough change in behavior to minimize infections because there are numerous factors such as poverty and lack of individual power in making decisions about one's sexuality that work against expected behavior change. In certain contexts, however, having knowledge of HIV/AIDS and its mode of transmission may present a new kind of challenge. Anthropologist Shanti Parikh, who works on HIV/AIDS in Uganda, notes that Uganda's success in anti-AIDS campaigns that led to significant drops in infection rates in the 1990s may have been its own undoing as reports of increased infections are emerging: "Uganda's HIV prevention messages may be inadvertently contributing to increased difficulty in acknowledging HIV risk and to newer forms of sexual secrecy" (2007, 1198).

Uganda's anti-HIV campaigns of the 1980s and 1990s brought sex into the public domain and offered ways to reduce sexual risk but "did not talk directly about the sexual acts themselves" (Parikh 2005, 125). In this way, the connection between HIV and sex was a bit removed from the everyday knowledge absorbed and managed by many people, especially the youth. People could talk about the connection between HIV and sex but not in concrete terms acknowledging the emotions linked to sexuality that could lead to the risky

behavior the anti-AIDS campaigns target. This dilemma between public messages and individual response to the messages is not lost to Wagosi wa Kaya,
who recommend that HIV/AIDS education become a part of elementary-
school curriculum. They say that HIV/AIDS education should be taught in
every school, because many people do not want to even confront the reality of
AIDS as carried in newspapers or billboards. Information about HIV/AIDS
has saturated the minds of many East Africans to an extent that many ignore
or all together avoid any information related to HIV/AIDS. In the same song,
Wagosi wa Kaya sing of this troubling reality:

> When someone buys a newspaper to read
> And sees some news on AIDS, he/she skips that page quickly
> And chooses to read about soccer results or politics
> Now tell me, is that really smart?
> What is shocking is that people are not afraid of HIV/AIDS

That "people are not afraid of HIV/AIDS" may be evident in the rising
reports of infidelity and risky sexual behavior. The threat of the disease on
individual lives seems to be low, as Parikh continues to show in the case of
Uganda, where many married men are more worried about getting caught
in extramarital affairs than in contracting HIV/AIDS: "[R]ecent notions of
sexual immorality have altered the social acceptability of infidelity, heighten-
ing men's personal motivation for sexual secrecy to avoid public scorn and
domestic conflict. Risk in this sense, is more about the social risk of getting
caught in sexual scandals, and less about the biomedical risk of catching a
sexually transmitted infection" (2007, 1199).

Similar observations regarding sexual risk are noted in a study by a group
from the Medical Research Council Programme on AIDS/Uganda Virus Research Institute (MRC/UVRI) in Entebbe, Uganda. One observation is, "[E]
very year since 2000, there's been an increase, at least in the rural population cohort, in the percentage of men aged 40 and above who have claimed
to have had two or more casual partners in the last month. That percentage
has increased since the year 2000. So there are some other sexual behavior
indicators that we looked at, such as condom use, which doesn't appear to
have changed very much. In young men, age 16, the percentage of 16 year
olds who have ever had sex has increased a bit since 2000 as well" (Leigh
Shafer, qtd. in Marco and Bernard 2007).

It is not my intention here to argue that persistence and spread of HIV/
AIDS are a result of an information deficit but rather to show that such information, the way it is delivered, and the consequences it produces, especially

given prevailing sociocultural contexts, elicits unexpected outcomes. Many of the men Shanti Parikh writes about are not at risk of HIV/AIDS due to their socioeconomic constraints (poverty and lack of HIV/AIDS awareness) that greatly contribute to the spread of the disease. They are rather more concerned about the social risk of HIV/AIDS. Moreover, as antiretroviral (ARV) drugs continue to be available to many more people, there is the risk of seeing such drugs as the cure for AIDS that would lead many to relax their campaign for prevention. There is also another danger, that of primarily linking HIV/AIDS with promiscuity. When and if people find out that they have HIV/AIDS, they do not want to be public about it because of the stigma that accompanies such a revelation, because besides being seen as promiscuous, they are also shunned and treated like outcasts by community members and even their own families.

Stigma, Testing, and People Living with AIDS

While certain perceptions, assumptions, and attitudes regarding people with HIV/AIDS have changed, a lot of stigma still accompanies those with the disease. In the song "Msinitenge," Professor Jay narrates the ordeal that a person with HIV/AIDS has to go through each day. He starts the song by playing the role of a person with AIDS:

> I confess that I have been infected with AIDS
> My journey has come to an end, and I am suffering greatly
> My health is deteriorated, I have diarrhea, and I am vomiting
> I am on my knees praying, aware that my day is coming
> After taking a test I knew I was not okay
> Now I have a role to notify the entire population

Many campaigns for HIV/AIDS awareness have emphasized the need to be public about one's status so as to reduce the rate of new infections. Billboards and messages on public transportation encourage people to get tested and know their status. Some churches have asked their pastors to require HIV/AIDS testing for all couples intending to have their marriages conducted in those churches. These efforts must be applauded and supported because once one knows his/her HIV/AIDS status, it becomes easier to reduce that person's rate of infecting others either by choosing to abstain from sex or by using protection. Knowing one's status also allows for one to have early access to ARVs, which can lead to a longer normal life. While all this "openness" about one's HIV/AIDS status is important, the reality is that one runs the risk of being shunned and socially isolated, as Professor Jay points out in the following excerpt from "Msinitenge":

> What I did was share my news about my AIDS status
> Then many looked at me with disdain just because I have AIDS
> And then they claim that every AIDS victim must have contracted it
>   through sex
> This is why I have decided to come out and speak openly
> Many forget that AIDS is also transmitted through injections
> Razor blades and scissors at the hospital are other examples

Responding to this social stigma directed at people living with HIV/AIDS is a major challenge for caregivers and policy makers alike. The emphasis that Professor Jay places on other forms of transmission is a reference to the common association between HIV/AIDS and promiscuity and the stigma that results from such an association. This stigma is also extended to children whose parents die of AIDS as Professor Jay continues to show:

> Children get AIDS from their parents
> But when their parents die, the community abandons them
> This happens both at home and in school
> My sympathies go to all those who are shunned in public

While African communities are known for their extended family networks and even the adage that "it takes a village to raise a child," numerous orphans now live in East Africa. Many of these orphans are often publicly identified as AIDS orphans and mostly shunned and neglected because of their status. Childcare is primarily undertaken by women in East Africa as in other parts of the world. As more women continue to be infected with the disease due to lack of individual and social power as well as little or no economic independence, the number of orphans will continue to grow. As the economic, social, and emotional drain of HIV/AIDS on individuals, families, and communities grows and continues to be heavily felt by women due to their sociocultural status, more and more strategies have to be realized that will assist them directly and holistically.

As Professor Jay further shows, it is hard for people living with AIDS to get any sympathy or support from family members or even health-care providers. This neglect has devastating psychological effects in the victims as well. In the summer of 2006 while visiting with Professor Jay in Dar es Salaam, we had a chance to talk about the reception his songs have among some of the audience members. He mentioned, for instance, that he received numerous thanks from

many people living with HIV/AIDS who had heard his song "Msinitenge."
Many, he said, expressed their gratitude, especially for the clarity with which
he portrayed their plight and his ability to give an empathetic face and voice
to those living with the disease.[11] The following excerpt from the song may
explain this response from people living with HIV/AIDS:

> When I go to the hospital, people stare at me
> When I am unable to walk, nurses insult me
> My body is weak and I am all smelly
> Who is going to touch me and at least cover me with a bedsheet?
> When I ask for assistance, everybody looks the other side
> Please scratch me even if it is with a stick

This song gives a real image of suffering from the victim's perspective, the
struggles one has with physical pain as well as social isolation. In many cases,
much of the discourse on HIV/AIDS tends to be centered on what people
with the virus need to do. In this case, Professor Jay provides the victims'
perspective and how they experience the disease. Because of fear of contracting AIDS as well as the shame that accompanies the assumed mode of transmission, it has been very hard to actually consider people living with AIDS
as deserving or desiring similar treatment to that given their counterparts
who do not have HIV/AIDS. This leads Professor Jay to challenge society:

> Many of you despise people living with AIDS
> You laugh at me and yet you do not go to get tested
> If you really care about yourselves, then get tested and know your status
> Save the next generation by getting tested

Professor Jay is showing that people still despise people living with AIDS
and that many do not even want to know their own HIV/AIDS status.
Knowing one's status may lead to taking specific steps such as abstinence
or condom use.

As it is with many social factors, there are mixed messages given by hip
hop artistes regarding condom use. Indeed, it is not quite clear how much
has changed in terms of reducing HIV/AIDS infection rates due to the use
of condoms. Many hip hop artistes, therefore, promote the use of condoms
while others warn that condoms are not the solution. In the song "Juala,"
Circute and Jo-el say:

> Check out these facts and figures, five hundred people die daily
> As if they are being crushed by motor vehicles

And then you want sex without protection. I am against that!
I am opposed to that, you fool
I am opposed to sex without protection

In his song "Mwekume (Guard yourself)," Uganda's Bobi Wine asks young people to use condoms if they cannot abstain from sex. In the video version of the song, Bobi Wine is seen distributing condoms to groups of youth in various parts of Kampala and shows clips of other popular hip hop artistes asking people to use condoms. These clips start with one by the late Philly Lutaaya, a famous *kadongo kamu* musician from Uganda, who is one of the very few musicians I know to have come out openly and declare his HIV-positive status in the 1980s. He also had a documentary—*Born in Africa*—made of his final days. Lutaaya died in 1989 at the height of HIV/AIDS infection in Uganda. He helped sensitize the society on the dangers of the disease by traveling all over Uganda with the message that AIDS was transmitted through sexual contact. I remember watching the documentary and becoming really afraid of HIV/AIDS. Whatever fear of HIV I hold up to date emanates from the message I received after watching the documentary featuring Lutaaya's life as he died of AIDS. The documentary continues to be a powerful tool for sensitizing many people on the reality of the disease. This may point to the power of visual media and real-life narratives in communicating clearly the real threat of HIV/AIDS. Using music to talk about abstinence and condom use is a good medium that can reach many people. In contributing to this reality, Bobi Wine uses "Mwekume" to ask people to become faithful to their partners. He specifically asks men to be faithful to their partners:

You can't be a real man if you don't respect your woman's life
And you can't respect your woman's life when you don't protect it
Use a condom and you will be safe

Such a message may be an important part of expanding the discourse on sexuality but has to be looked at in light of reports of increased sexual activity and with multiple partners. Even the message of condom use should not be seen as a foolproof protection against HIV/AIDS and other sexually transmitted diseases, as Professor Jay shows in "Msinitenge":

Who told you condoms prevent AIDS?
I see you are fighting a losing battle
AIDS cannot be prevented not even with metal condoms
The only way out is to be faithful to your partner

Clearly, these are mixed messages being sent out regarding strategies to combat the spread of HIV/AIDS. Should it be abstinence, condom use, and/or staying faithful to one's partner? How feasible is each method, anyway? It seems that each person, community, and society has to have an approach that best suits its context. But in all approaches, communication and information sharing regarding the disease and its attendant contexts have to be central. Some hip hop artistes have tried to step into the scene as victims of HIV/AIDS in order to communicate to their audience members the dangers of HIV/AIDS. The song "Vumilia (Persevere)" performed by seven famous hip hop artistes in Kenya (Attitude, Bamboo, Doobiez, Jua Cali, Mercy Myra, Nonini, and Tattuu) in 2005 and sponsored by Program for Appropriate Technology in Health (PATH) in Nairobi, is such an example. The song was composed especially to warn the youth against reckless sexual lives that could expose them to HIV/AIDS as well as the dangers of trying to emulate the lives the musicians present through their music:

> There are some young people who want to be like us
> [Saying] "Mom, Mom, I want to have dreaded hair like that of Nazizi"
> That is okay but remember music is just entertainment
> What you see on video is just acting and does not reflect our real lives
> If you agree with Bishop Ndingi [of the Catholic Church] then abstain
> If you have a girlfriend, be faithful to her
> And if you like sex, then use a condom

This approach that places all the three options together seems to go well with the reality that no single method will be the answer to the HIV/AIDS problem. Other strategies that hip hop artistes use involve narratives that include the musicians themselves as the victims of AIDS. In a composition that won the 2005 song of the year in Tanzania's Kilimanjaro Awards and BBC's male artiste of the year award, Tanzania's Ferooz Mrisho plays the role of a promiscuous young man who ends up getting infected with HIV/AIDS and narrates his ordeal from his deathbed. In the song "Starehe (Pleasure)," Ferooz clearly narrates how he used to have multiple partners and never used protection because he thought condoms would inhibit his sexual pleasure:

> I changed girls like they were public transport vehicles
> I chased all women, prostitutes, high-class women, and low-class
>   women alike
> I wanted to have all the fun
> I did not have time to even remember my God . . .

Now here I am on my deathbed
Pleasure has led me astray and now I will never be well again

What is interesting, however, is that the narrative is about the man dying of AIDS after he has had many female partners, and none of his female partners are represented as having suffered the same ordeal. In this way, HIV/AIDS infection is presented as emanating from the woman (women) and then to the man and not the other way round even when reports from some East African communities indicate that because of women's weakened economic and social power, they are more likely to be infected by their partners and especially by husbands (Carpenter et al. 1999; Clark 2004). Further, audience members are not given an opportunity to empathize or feel the pain that female partners feel, as in the case of the man. The women are left without a voice and only projected as the evil behind the man's suffering. When asked whether the song "Starehe" was a real-life experience he was narrating, Ferooz said, "This is a real-life experience, especially the fact that I have lost a considerable number of very close friends and relatives. I saw the need of the public to know that AIDS is real and is going to wipe out the next generation if caution is not taken. AIDS is real and never witchcraft, and it pains me when I see a young person succumb to this scourge."[12]

It seems as if the message of the song got to the audience members as it was intended to because many people thought that Ferooz, like Lutaaya, was playing out his real- life experiences. This led to some people assuming that he was HIV positive, because he says in the interview, "I have lots of friends who come to me to find out whether I am positive as the video I caricatured an HIV/AIDS victim. So most people are wondering whether I am sick. Nope. I shot the video in hospital [because] I wanted to pass the message well and so I got all types of friends [to assist me]."[13]

As experts, communities, and governments continue to grapple with the challenges brought by AIDS, it is increasingly becoming clear that the poor are suffering the most. Without new ways of addressing their structural marginality, the challenges of HIV/AIDS will continue to grow. Moreover, with increased poverty come fewer options for living a healthy lifestyle, which often leads to some patients selling their ARVs in order to buy food as was reported of some HIV/AIDS victims in Kenya (Ngesa 2007). In the final analysis, increasing HIV/AIDS awareness has to be matched by improving socioeconomic status and reducing the imbalance in power between women and men. Such changes will require policies that are designed to avail resources to all communities in order to raise their standard of living, empower women, and make available different methods of protection during sex. Policies that, for instance, aim to decrease the gender gap in education, improve women's access to economic resources, increase women's political participation, and protect women from violence will be especially key in empowering women. Further, a concerted effort by communities to publicly discuss sex and sexuality will increase the chances of information sharing and breaking the code of silence, especially for women and girls. The reality of increased sexual activity among youth of all walks of life has to be countered with sex education at all levels of society and in the prominent social institution such as schools, religious communities, and at home. I have shown that hip hop has provided an opportunity to start making positive steps towards more communication and discourse on sexuality. In playing their part, musicians have also to continually warn their audience members against ignoring the threat of HIV/AIDS and other sexually transmitted diseases.

6

Staying True to the Cause
Hip Hop's Enduring Social Role

I can authoritatively say that hip hop saved me. . . .
It kept me away from bad groups and helped me further
my education; my message has thereafter been that
urban youth should embrace positive hip hop.

—Gidi Gidi, of Gidi Gidi Maji Maji

Contemporary globalization and the sociopolitical ramifications that accompany it have greatly asserted their influence on the political, economic, and cultural terrain in East Africa. The advent of hip hop music in East Africa is itself a result of this globalizing process. Granted that the expressive form of hip hop adopted by East African youth in the process of negotiating identity in this globalizing context is quite similar to U.S. rap and hip hop, I have argued here that the content and shape of this hip hop are localized to reflect East African realities and sensibilities. Hip hop as performed and composed in East Africa embodies key discourses about African identity, about postcolonial experiences of modernity, and about sociocultural changes that result from multiple factors that interact with the lived experiences of many of the youth performing it. Through the lyrics and choice of specific metaphors of representation, East African hip hop brings together artistes' own historical past within current global realities and then creatively weaves them into a critique of the prevailing sociocultural reality. Hip hop also allows youth to step into a social space through which they question the global framework of inequality with which their nations are faced while also celebrating and taking advantage of certain opportunities opened up by the same process of globalization. Hip hop is crucial in defining and redefining this complex interaction that youth have with globalization as well as in delineating their identities in a postcolonial polity that is itself struggling to create a unique local identity while navigating an overwhelming global presence.

Since the birth of the modern nation-state in East Africa, youth have had very limited opportunities for self-actualization and expression in public. With the entry of hip hop into the public sphere, however, many youth have inserted themselves into the public arena through social commentary and critique. East African artists have strategically appropriated, adapted, and combined what would be considered "foreign" influences and cultural artifacts together with "local" ones in order to celebrate their cultures, redefine localities, and accentuate their African identities as they attempt to define those same African identities. I have also argued and shown that hip hop has become an important platform through which youth can articulate political issues affecting them in ways that no other medium could readily avail to them. Hip hop has also become a mouthpiece through which youth engage and get involved in critiquing the social, cultural, and political realities of their time.

Hip hop music is arguably the fastest-growing component of youth culture in Africa today. Its rapid growth and acceptance in all parts of Africa can be attributed to a number of factors, including but not limited to its ability to be localized through style and content, its role in creating opportunities for youth to insert themselves in the public space through a medium they can locally negotiate, and the opportunities for economic advancement to which otherwise disenfranchised youth have access. In all these opportunities, what stands out is the role played by hip hop in articulating, shaping, and projecting youth identities in ways that were hitherto publicly unavailable to many of them. For a number of these youth, earlier definitions of who they are have been reconfigured and reconstituted into new expressions that are conscious of the prevailing local realities and the youth's own aspirations. As the nation-state retreats from its role as an agent for socialization, youth in East Africa have been left to define, design, and implement their own model of who they are and want to be both in private and public spaces. In the process, they have borrowed from multiple sources and produced a tapestry of identities reflective of their sociopolitical times. They have also transcended the common geographic boundaries of nation-state that are often used to define and analyze their music and identities and performed music that extends beyond established political and ethnic boundaries.

Indeed, as shown throughout the current volume, none of the artists whose work is analyzed have, for instance, any distinct Kenyan, Ugandan, or Tanzanian identity. By virtue of the language and content of their music, the relative ease with which this music travels across national boundaries, increased collaboration in producing and performing songs, and their lived experiences in a sociocultural context in which there are shared political and economic experiences, it is hard to limit or even link them to a specific national or ethnic location. The musicians themselves seem aware of the porous nature of the existing political boundaries. In a 2005 interview for www. musicuganda.com, Uganda's Chameleone stated, "One thing we must realize as entertainers in the region is that there are no borders anymore. We must work together as one to take music and entertainment to new levels. That is the only way music is going to be of use to our people in East Africa."[1]

Hence, it may have been a surprise to many East Africans that Chameleone is Ugandan and not Kenyan. That Chameleone made his name as a musician in Nairobi when he recorded with Kenya's Ogopa DJs defines him more as a Kenyan than Ugandan. Chameleone also sings mostly in Kiswahili rather than in Luganda, a language that is used by many other Ugandan musicians. In this way, many see him as an artiste from Kenya than Uganda, where there is minimal use of Swahili. The incident mentioned in chapter 1 in which Chameleone, along with Kenya's Redsan, were invited to curtain-raise for raga music star Shaggy during his Bombastic Kenya Tour in 2002, is evidence of this identity mix-up. Some of the organizers for the event had assumed that Chameleone was Kenyan and invited him to perform as a way of showcasing Kenya's musical talent. This may reflect the cosmopolitan nature of hip hop itself as well as the artistes' abilities to transcend national boundaries in defining themselves, their lyrics, and styles of music.

One cannot easily confine East African hip hop to style, content, or identity that is located in one geographic space or link it to a specific ethnic group. It is a music that transcends arbitrary national political boundaries and ethnicized cultural experiences. Hip hop song lyrics are often composed to reflect regional or cosmopolitan identities in the musicians and their fans and transcends received moral boundaries. Moreover, the songs make direct reference to the lives of urbanized East African youth by using an idiom that mobilizes images, words, and references specific to their lived and imagined realities that are often unbounded by spatial and temporal realities. Through hip hop East African youth have also penetrated public discourse in telling ways.

Unlike in past generations when music performed in public was composed in a language palatable to all audiences, contemporary Western-media-influenced youth are not shy to use direct language in addressing issues that challenge moral boundaries in the case of sex and sexuality in the context of HIV/AIDS. Themes of ribald sexuality and social issues regarding unemployment, teenage pregnancies, and neocolonialism often find expression in the same context in a way helping define the identities and experiential realities of hip hop's practitioners. What is more, these are exactly the same social realities facing the youth. Hip hop has availed to a new brand of East Africans the opportunity to challenge representations of Africa and, in turn, represent their voices that have seldom been heard in public discourse on African identity. When multinational corporations take over local businesses and exploit local resources, hip hop artistes are at hand to report and challenge them in public. When people living with AIDS are neglected and mistreated at health facilities, hip hop artistes compose and perform songs to expose and castigate such abuse.

In his song "Shida zetu za Kawaida (Our normal problems)," Muki Garang from Kenya attempts to address this role played by hip hop when he talks about the challenges facing Africa and Africans today:

> Africa is the name of this continent
> You will see poverty in every corner, war from Sierra Leone to Somalia
> And both adults and children dying of malaria
> As the old and youth like me struggle to avoid HIV/AIDS

This is the common image that we get of Africa from most of Western media and even private expressions. It is an image of Africa as a "dark" continent, riddled with disease, war, and drought. Is Garang reproducing that same caricature of Africa, or is he giving us an honest depiction of the continent? The next few lines answer this question:

> There is technology all over and when I watch television
> I realize that other people don't live like this
> I heard that being born with a black skin is similar to being cursed
> I say forget all that, a human being is a human being

It is interesting that he blends a depiction of the reality of an Africa that is different from "other" places with a philosophical and even cosmological explanation for Africa's predicament in which Blackness is seen as a consequence of supernatural powers. Although a number of interpretations can come out of these words, I argue that Garang brings out the complexity of understanding African sociopolitical and economic realities. He does so by appealing to already existing public discourse on Africa but also on competing realities of where Africa is in reality or imagination. He then turns to the role of the hip hop artiste:

> I only have a mike in my hand trying to avoid poverty and HIV/AIDS
> When one is poor, it is almost as if one is ill
> I try my best to earn an honest living

I will not sell my soul in order to make it
I will not sing nonsense so as to be played on radio

Instructively, Garang addresses one of the dilemmas that may face a number of East African hip hop artistes—should they stay true to their social messages and have little airplay and popularity or sing about sex and partying and sell more records? These are the challenges artistes such as Ukooflani Mau Mau and Wagosi wa Kaya often face because FM radio stations tend to play songs that have less socially serious messages. Despite the powerful role hip hop plays in challenging social ills and representing youth identity, the artistes have to grapple with the real issue of making a living from their art. Further, they have to live up with the challenges of the legitimacy of hip hop as a respectable medium through which artistes can make a livelihood and articulate serious social issues.

For many East Africans, music making, including its performance and consumption, has the connotations of vagrancy or laziness, and it is often associated with mischief, especially when performed by youth. Some hip hop artistes are responsible for this negative image because as Garang says above, they are willing to "sing nonsense so as to be played on radio." There is in a way a genuine reason for this attitude by some artistes. As I have argued elsewhere,

> [D]ue to the structural organization of paid work in our cultures, music consumption has been restricted to periods that are characterized with the absence of structured work; music consumption is often a leisure activity restricted to periods when people are not at work. Moreover, due to the dispersed living set-ups in cities and some rural areas, group consumption of music on a regular basis is restricted to social spaces marked as leisure spots (such as beerhalls and clubs) where music production and consumption is accompanied by the sale of beer and other beverages. It is this background of time and space allocation that gives music its social meaning and status. (1999, 34)

This association of music consumption with certain social spaces and times has made it difficult for many East Africans, who for the most part have been socialized to a capitalist ethic of equating "real work" with formal employment in an office, professional activities such as teaching, nursing, and accounting, or agricultural activities. Indeed, until recently (when music started becoming a legitimate source of livelihood and as a platform for social commentary), performing popular music had been regarded as the work of idle and socially wayward individuals.

Kenya's hip hop music got a real boost of legitimacy when Fernando Meire-lles award-winning movie *The Constant Gardener* featured the song "Forever" by the group Necessary Noize. Furthermore, many government agencies and nongovernmental organizations have realized the power of hip hop in reaching and communicating directly with the youth who in East Africa constitute more than half of the populations. In Tanzania, the work of Professor Jay has placed hip hop on a high social status after he was nationally recognized for his song "Ndio Mzee." For some, as in the Kenyan political scene (chapter 4), the youth are a viable mass that can be appropriated and mobilized for political expediency. But this becomes a double-edged sword that cuts both ways as the youth also use hip hop to jump-start their political campaigns.

Quite often, critics and pundits will claim that popular culture pollutes and contaminates the youth (Dolby 2006), especially because of its association with Westernization that is often seen as a model of moral decadence. Because of hip hop's earlier association with gangster rap from the United States, some East Africans still regard it as "bad" music. Writing about Tanzanian hip hop and identity, Alex Perullo notes, "[M]any rappers and rap fans are labeled *wahuni* [hooligans], and rap has been perceived as a music corrupting the minds of the country's young" (2005, 76). But as Professor Jay says in a mock interview with a political leader in a segment of the album *Machozi, Jasho, na Damu*, "Rap music is not music by hooligans. It conveys messages of political, social, and economic reality." This statement points to two important threads in understanding hip hop's place in the social terrain of East Africa's moral terrain. First, it negates the perceived identity of hip hop musicians as hooligans. Second, it calls upon musicians to refrain from making hip hop a medium for expressing hooliganism.

Local hip hop artistes who want to display a larger-than-life image of themselves have been criticized by fellow musicians. Tanzania's Afande Sele in his song "Kioo cha Jamii (Social mirror)" says that an artiste is a society's mirror that sees far and deep. He castigates his fellow rappers who want to project a make-believe lifestyle, talking about having a Mercedes Benz while they live in a mud hut. He says that people need to hear serious messages, not messages about self, alcohol, and sex, especially in an era of AIDS and in one of the poorest countries in the world. But the beauty of expressive culture is that it has both the good and the bad, and only the consumers can truly decide the quality of the music and messages.

When 50 Cent or Kanye West have a fight over who is the most popular hip hop artiste in the United States or when they release a new song, East African artistes will know at the same time as their North American counterparts. East African youth may even buy or illegally download the music and sing along when it is played on radio. However, many of them understand the socioeconomic differences attendant in these two locations, and only imagined realities can bring them together (see Weiss 2002). What they do is straddle both worlds—the global and the local—simultaneously to produce a music that is informed by both worlds but that mostly represents the local. As shown in this book, the local is not necessarily tied to the nation-state within which the artist operates but rather because, and not in spite of, the global flavor the music is extranational. Mbugua wa Mungai puts it clearly: "[Y]outh [hip hop] culture trains its gaze outwards from the local to the global in order for them to look back into the local" (2007, 48).

This increased flow and contact between the local and the global have their own nagging outcomes as well. The flurry of cultural goods brought by contemporary globalization, for instance, may account for an emerging group of East African hip hop artistes who may clamor for the same glamour of bling bling and fancy cars that is displayed by U.S. hip hop artistes, as in the case of Kenya's CMB Prezzo, discussed in chapter 2. Yet, because of their material realities and the increased presence of opportunities for social critique and commentary, many East African hip hop artistes have used hip hop as an important platform to assert their role as contemporary players in their societies that are facing major socioeconomic and political challenges. Unlike the common view held by many politicians, these youth are not the leaders of tomorrow but are ready to take on positions of leadership. They have the determination and skills necessary for such leadership. By using hip hop as an avenue through which to access this readiness, I am arguing for an analysis of social reality through different media and especially media that is also available locally. As the fastest-growing mode of youth communication and expression, hip hop has a definite place in the ethnography of contemporary East Africa's sociopolitical and economic realities. This reality is articulated well by the group Ukooflani Mau Mau:

> The objectives of the group are quality enhancement to enable hip-hop to be the language to pass the real/true message to society. Through enlightening people on the economic prospects of hip-hop they'd like to prove its viability as a business and a way to sustain an income for fellow youth from disadvantaged backgrounds. UFMM believe hip-hop is a tested and proven way out of the ghetto because it has been their rehabilitation. Coming from an environment where it is an achievement to see the age of 25, and where an average person earns less that $1 a day; UFMM happily prove that with wit, clever poetry, leadership, wisdom and love, one can control their destiny.[2]

Hip hop will continue to play a major role in the social lives of many East Africans. In some instances, it has become the new medium that youth are using to redefine external images and definitions of Africa. With films dedicated to hip hop music in East Africa such as *Shika, Hip Hop Colony,* and *Hali Halisi,* as well as numerous video and audio music sources on Youtube and at www.africanhiphop.com, I am sure East African hip hop will continue to gain presence not only in East Africa but across the world.

Appendix: Hip Hop Artistes

This summary of hip hop artistes is a small representation of information available publicly on the Worldwide Web and for some artistes knowledge gathered by the author from interacting with them. A Google search brings up numerous entries for all these artistes, and readers are invited to find more about the artistes on the artistes' personal Web sites. Most of the information was retrieved from www.africanhiphop.com, www.ugpulse.com, www.ukooflanimaumau.com, and www.musicuganda.com.

Afande Sele: Born Selemani Msindi, Afande Sele is a former soldier who turned to hip hop through association with Joseph Mbilinyi (another hip hop artiste once known as Mr. II and later Sugu). Sele initially was featured in the track "Siku Nikianguka (The day I fall)" performed by Sugu later collaborated with other artistes including Jay Mo in his first single, "Mayowe (Screams)." In 2002, Sele released his first album *Mkuki Moyoni* (Spear in the heart), then *Darubini Kali* (Strong telescope) in 2004, which contains the songs "Kioo cha Jamii (Social mirror)" and "Nafsi ya Mtu (One's selfhood)" in 2006. Unlike most Tanzanian artists, who moved to Dar es Salaam for greener pastures, Sele has made his native town of Morogoro his operating base. He is one of the few consistent musicians singing about serious social issues.

Bebe Cool: Born Moses Ssali, he is regarded by many as the "bad boy" of popular music in Uganda because he seems to draw controversy all the time. Starting his music career in Kenya with Redsan and Chameleone, Bebe Cool has maintained his East African reach by incorporating Kenyan musicians into what they refer to as the East African Bashment Crew. He says that his music is inspired by current events and personal experiences. Besides singing, Bebe Cool provides instrumentation and produces his music. His song "Sikiliza (Listen)" is from his *Maisha* (Life) album produced by Bava Studios in 2004.

Bobi Wine: Born in Kamwokya, in one of the worst slums of Kampala, Uganda, Kyagulanyi Sentamu Robert (Bobi Wine) has tasted the tough urban life many musicians try to depict in their music. This, however, did not deter him from pursuing a passion he had for music especially reggae, which he has localized into an Afro pop that has made him quite popular in East Africa. Locally referred to as His Excellency, Bobi won the 2006 Pearl of Africa Music (PAM) Artist of the Year award. He leads the Fire Basement Crew, based in Kamwokya, which seeks to fight on behalf of people living in ghettoes, not only in Uganda but all over the world. Bobi is a graduate of Makerere University where he earned a degree in music, dance, and drama. His songs include "Adam ne Kawa (Adam and Eve)" from his *Taata wa'baana* (Children's father) album (2005) and "Mwekume (Guard yourself)" recorded in the album *Mwekume* (2003). He has done commercials for Ugandan companies such as Centenary Bank Limited, Lifeguard Condoms, Aqua Safe companies, and MTN Uganda.

Chameleone: Joseph Mayanja, a.k.a. Chameleone, is one of the most popular and successful musicians in East Africa today. He has traveled and performed extensively having started his career in Nairobi after trying his hand in local clubs in Kampala, Uganda, and Rwanda. While in Nairobi, he linked up with Bebe Cool and Redsan and came up with "Mikono juu (Hands up)," which became a number-one hit single on East Africa Radio. He then wrote and recorded "Bageya" (name of a person in Luganda) with Redsan, which, although sung in Luganda, became number one in Nairobi with it being played on all radio stations and discos. He returned to Kampala, where he continued to record and produce hit after hit and has now become one of the most sought-after musicians in East Africa. His song "Mama Mia" appears in his *Mama Mia* album (2001).

Circute and Jo-el: This duo of cousins whose only successful time together was with the song "Juala" (local slang for plastic bag, which in this case denotes a condom). They seem to have disappeared as quickly as they appeared on the public scene.

Deux Vultures: A two-man show—Thomas Konzanga a.k.a. Nasty Thomas and Daudi Mustapha a.k.a. Colonel Moustapha—who have become very popular in East Africa for their danceable tunes. They made their entry into the hip hop scene when they were signed on by Kenya's most successful DJs—Ogopa Dee Jays—and included in Ogopa's first hip hop compilation with their song "Mona Lisa" in 2002. The song was so popular that it was played in almost all dance clubs and radio stations in East Africa. The group released other hit songs, such as "Katika (Dance)," "Kinyaunyau" (local coinage for a high-maintenance woman), and "Adhiambo C" (female name among the Luo), with Calif Records and earned many music awards including Kenya's Kisima and South Africa's Kora.

Ferooz Mrisho: Although often known for performing with other artistes such as Professor Jay, Ferooz Mrisho is a member of the Dar es Salaam hip-hop group Daz Nundaz that was formed in the mid-nineties. The group came to the limelight when they released a single "Kamanda" and were offered a contract to record a full album at Bongo Records studios. However, the members of the group have ever since done solo performances and recordings. Ferooz recorded his solo album *Safari* produced by P Funk (Bongo Records) which features the song "Starehe (Pleasure)," which he performed with Professor Jay. Ferooz won the Kilimanjaro Music Award for Best Single 2004 as well as BBC Tanzania Award for Best Male Bongo Flava Artist.

Kalamashaka: Started in 1995 and comprising three musicians—Kamau, John, and Robert—Kalamashaka is the pioneer hip hop group in Kenya. Their hit single "Tafsiri Hii (Translate this)," a hit in 1997, placed them squarely in Africa's hip hop scene. Their first album, *Ni Wakati* (2001), was well received in East Africa and spread elsewhere especially when South Africa's Channel O played *Fanya Mambo* (Do something), a video from the album. Even with the expansion of free speech and the increase in commercial FM stations, Kalamashaka's music, which is always about the reality of the struggles many face in poverty, was rarely played publicly. They soon were surpassed by newer artistes who became popular by playing entertainment music. However, Kalamashaka's dedication to social issues saw them collaborate with other artistes to form Ukooflani Mau Mau, and the two together released *Kilio Cha Haki* (Cry of justice) album (2004), followed by *Dandora Burning* (2006). Both albums present issues facing the youth in a corrupt and at times repressive government.

Lady Jaydee: Born Judith Daines Wambura, Lady Jaydee is one of the most famous Tanzanian artistes today. Voted Best Tanzanian Female R&B artist in 2002 in Tanzania and given an award for the Best Female Video in South Africa in 2005, she has positioned herself as one major player in the East African hip hop scene. Her career started as a presenter at Tanzania's Clouds 88.4 FM radio station, one of the major promoters of local music in Tanzania. She recorded two songs—"Nakupenda (I love you)" and "Mpenzi Wangu (My love)" in 2000—while working for the radio station. Following the success of these two singles, she quit her radio stint to fully pursue a music career. Her song "Wanaume kama mabinti (Men who are like women)" (2003) in the album *Binti* (Daughter or young woman) by MJ Productions situated her as a social critic. In July 2007, her song "Siku Hazigandi (Days do not linger forever)" was number one on South Africa's Channel O.

Mesach Semakula: Performing what he considers Afro Pop, Semakula is best known for his music videos in which he reenacts real-life scenarios as he sings. At sixteen, he joined the Emitone band led by the late Umaru Katumba, but he was too young and was asked to leave the band. At eighteen, he teamed up with Geoffrey Lutaaya and Ronald Mayinja but later broke off from the group to go solo and start his own recording studio in Kampala. His song "First Aid" (2006) by Dream Studios showcases his ability to explore male-female relations in a fresh way.

Mr. Ebbo: Abel Loshilaa Motika (Mr. Ebbo) is from the Arusha ethnic group that is culturally very close to the Maasai. He has taken up this cultural proximity to cut out an image of a Maasai warrior for himself when he performs his music. He started his music career in Arusha singing and performing reggae sounds and then switched to local R&B, and again switched, this time to rap. He moved to Tanga and produces his own music under Motika Records. He is best known for dressing up like a Maasai and singing with a Maasai accent especially in his song "Mi Mmasai (I am Maasai)," "Fahari Yako (Your pride)," and "Muwe na Huruma (Be merciful)" all in the *Fahari Yako* album (2000) by MJ Productions. In 2003, the Tanzanian government recruited Mr. Ebbo to compose a song to support the privatization project undertaken by the government. From this project came his single "Ubinafsishaji (Privatization)" that extols the virtues of private ownership.

Nonini: Born Hubert Nakitare, Nonini is probably best known for his explicit lyrics and made his real mark in hip hop with his 2002 single "Manzi wa Nairobi (Nairobi girl)." He is also associated with more-racy lyrics that border on profanity and seen as quite daring in terms of the themes he explores (almost always about male-female relationships).

Poxi Presh: His real name is Prechard Pouka Olang', and he came onto the Kenyan music scene in the 1990s with his popular songs "Otonglo Time" and "Salsa Afrique" that appear in the Nairobi City Ensemble compilation in the album *Kaboum Boum* (2005). He also featured prominently in a compilation by Nairobi City Ensemble that sought to celebrate Kenyan popular music with a blend of traditional tunes. Poxi is best remembered for fighting against music piracy and poor royalties paid to musicians by producers.

Professor Jay: Joseph Haule started as a rapper with the group Hardblasters in 2000, while using the name Nigga Jay. In 2001, he started a solo career by recording his 2001 album *Machozi, Jasho, na Damu* (tears, sweat, and blood), which was very successful in East Africa, especially his song "Ndio Mzee (Yes, sir)" that castigates politicians who will do anything to go to parliament. His 2003 album *Mapinduzi Halisi* (real revolution) features such songs as "Msinitenge (Do not abandon me)" and "Kikao cha Dharura (Emergency meeting)." He is one of the best composers of songs with rhyme and rhythm in East Africa. Singing in standard Kiswahili, Professor Jay has maintained his role as a voice of reason in a world often drawn to "feel good" songs.

Ukooflani Mau Mau: A conglomeration of groups that come together for different artistic projects of which music is a central one, the twenty-four-member clan comprises youth from the lower-class urban estates of Nairobi and Mombasa in Kenya and Tanzania from different ethnic backdrops and religious beliefs. The name *Ukooflani* is an acronym for *upendo kote olewenu ombeni funzo la aliyetuumba njia iwepo* (Love everywhere all who seek teachings of the creator, there is a way). According to their Web site, the objectives of the group are quality enhancement to enable hip hop to be the language to pass the real/true message to society (www.ukooflanimaumau.com). The song "All Over the World" (2004) in which they featured New York artist Rha

Goddess was their most widely received production. The song was part of a larger project with a group that was dubbed the *Nairobi Yetu Project* (our Nairobi project) to bring together many artistes from Nairobi to sing about social realities.

Wagosi wa Kaya: Two artists, Frederick Mariki a.k.a. Mkoloni and John Simba a.k.a. Dr. John, make up the group whose name comes from the Sambaa language, Tanzania, and means "home boys." They relate to the poor and disenfranchised because they mostly sing about problems facing common Tanzanians such as poor hospital conditions, retrenchment, police corruption, and privatization. So far, they have released three albums, *Ukweli Mtupu* (Real truth) (2001) with the songs "Titamtambuaje (How do we recognize him/her)," "Tumeshtuka (We are shocked)," and "Vinatia Uchungu (It is painful)"; *Ripoti Kamili* (Full report) (2003), and *Nyeti* (Serious) (2005).

Wahu Kagwi (Wahu): One of the few female artistes in Kenya who can stand up to the lyrical bullying of male artistes, Wahu started her singing while a student at Precious Blood Secondary School, Riruta (outside of Nairobi), and with a friend wrote her first song, "Showers of Blessings" as a tribute to God for the national academic success that their school enjoyed. Later, she recorded her first song *"Niangalie* (Look at me/watch over me)" that drew the attention of renowned Christian Broadcasting Network (CBN) presenter Victor Oladokun, who aired it on his *Turning Point* program. While a mathematics student at the University of Nairobi, Wahu managed to compose and record other songs but her real success came through her songs *"Liar,"* *"Sitishiki* (I am not impressed)," and *"Kibow Wow* (A man who lies about his success)," all of which continue to enjoy extensive airplay both locally and regionally. In November 2008, Wahu won the MTV Africa award for best song of the year with her song "Sweet Love."

Zay B: Born Zainab Lipangile, Zay B is a true feminist, singing specifically about the plight of women in Africa in general and Tanzania in particular. Her small stature does not compare with her loaded messages that often castigate women for not helping their lot when opportunity avails itself. Her hit single "Mama Africa" from her album with the same title was received well in the region and became a jingle for a program on women's issues on Tanzania public radio. Her songs "Monica" and "Akina Mama" (Women) appeared in her *Kufa na Kuzikana* (Dying and burying each other) album produced in 2004 and challenges women to use their own strategies toward gender equity rather than waiting for help from men.

Glossary

benga: A genre of popular music in Kenya often associated with the Luo people of Western Kenya. Originally performed on the Luo's eight-string lyre called *nyatiti*, benga music itself involves quick, syncopated melodies that involve the weaving of bass and rhythm guitars with the vocals. Kenya's popular music artistes from many parts of the country but especially those from the Kamba and Kikuyu ethnic groups, besides the Luo, have popularized this style of music.

bongo flava: Refers to Tanzania's popular music predominantly performed by the youth, which blends R&B, hip hop, and local musical styles. The term *bongo flava* comes from two words—*bongo,* a Kiswahili word for brains, and *flava,* a localized version of the English word *flavor.* In current usage, the word *bongo* refers to Tanzania's largest city, Dar es Salaam, to denote the need for one to use his/her brains to survive in the city, especially in the postsocialist era engulfed in private enterprise and individualism.

cavacha: A style of music common in Kenya but with heavy influence from Zairian rumba, which involves a fast-paced rhythm, played on a snare drum or high hat. Sometimes the beat is allowed to go on its own to intensify the dancing.

genge: A style of music common in Kenya that incorporates hip hop, dancehall, and traditional African music styles sung in Sheng (a blend of English, Kiswahili, and other local languages) and noted to have been popularized by the artiste Nonini. *Genge* is a Kiswahili word for *group of* or *mass* and often seen by some as carrying the connotations of *gang.*

kadongo kamu: A style of music popular in Uganda with a guitar and a vocalist as core performers. The words *kadongo kamu* literally mean "one-instrument performance," which has become quite popular in East Africa today. The singing in kadongo kamu is mostly based on long narratives about someone or the singer telling specific stories that the audience can connect with quickly.

kapuka: A style of music in Kenya often associated with hip hop artist Bamboo and other musicians from Nairobi's California Estate and is specifically known for its repeated beats and lyrics meant to enhance the song draw for dancing, and the name is attributed to a constant beat of kapu-kapu-kapu. Many sounds in kapuka are generated from existing computer tunes, and this makes many kapuka songs sound the same. California Estate is also associated with the birth of genge through Calif Records recording studio.

Notes

1. Globalization and Youth Agency in East Africa

1. Fred Mariki, telephone interview with author, December 12, 2007.

2. Ibid.

3. "Biographies—Chiz n Brain," Ukooflani Mau Mau, 2007, http://www .ukooflanimaumau.com/site/en/home/chizn_brain.html (accessed January 26, 2007).

4. Professor Jay, personal communication, June 23, 2006, Dar es Salaam, Tanzania.

5. Popular music has historically been seen as an art that draws the socially deviant, and, thus, many musicians have had to fight to defend their legitimate role as social critics. Professor Jay devotes a large portion of his album *Machozi, Jasho, na Damu* (Tears, sweat, and blood) to debunk the claims that *muziki wa rap ni uhuni* (rap music is for hooligans).

6. Fred Mariki, telephone interview with author, December 12, 2007. The awards ceremony for the competition took place at Mnazi Mmoja grounds in Dar es Salaam on December 8, 2007, and was attended by, among others, Zitto Kabwe, member of Parliament and director of the Office of International Affairs, who is locally known for his fight against corruption in Tanzania. In August 2007, for instance, he accused Nazir Karamagi, the minister for mining, of signing controversial mining contracts in London.

7. See "The University as a Site of Knowledge: The Role of Basic Research," Codesria, July 13, 2006, 2, available at www.codesria.org/Links/Publications/Chachage.pdf (accessed December 28, 2006).

8. Kenya's hip hop artistes Muki Garang and Ukooflani Mau Mau have popularized and distributed their music over the Internet because of their hard-hitting lyrics that are often not played by local radio station deejays.

9. See www.eac.int for more information regarding this regional intergovernmental organization that now has in its membership Burundi, Kenya, Rwanda, Tanzania, and Uganda.

2. Hip Hop and African Identity in Contemporary Globalization

1. "Hali Halisi Rap as an Alternative Medium," africanhiphop.com, November 10, 2004, available at www.africanhiphop.com/index.php?module=subjects&func=viewpage&pageid=220 (accessed January 21, 2006). Similar sentiments have been expressed by other East African artistes, including Xplastaz and Ukooflani Mau Mau.

2. In 1991, for instance, Swaleh J compiled an album titled *Swahili Rap*, which used Vanilla Ice's song "Ice Ice Baby" with Kiswahili lyrics. Hakim and Abdul through their musical group Contish followed suit by singing Kiswahili lyrics to the music of Shabba Ranks in Hakim and Abdul's album titled *Mabishoo* aptly called Swahili Rap and produced in 1993. In Kenya, DJs often recorded music on tape and sold it to willing buyers who were following the music scene closely. Florida 2000, a nightclub in Nairobi continually provided recorded music of the latest hits on Western music charts that was often sold in local stores.

3. See Carol Nyanga's article "The Fall and Fall of Kalamashaka," *Pulse Magazine, East African Standard,* February 20, 2004, for a full story of this rags-to-riches-to-rags story.

4. See "Tanzanian Hip Hop, the Old School (1991–1999)," africanhiphop.com, 2002, available at www.africanhiphop.com/index.php?module=subjects&func=printpage&pageid=100&scope=all (accessed April 3, 2004). Also see http://www.africaonline.co.tz/rockers/bprofiles2.htm for more information on this group.

5. "New Music Exiles Settle in Nairobi," special report, *Daily Nation,* March 17, 2004, 4. Many writers and commentators seem to favor writing about the educational achievements of successful hip hop stars in an attempt to dissuade the youth from seeing it as a genre for thugs as is often depicted in gangster rap.

6. See his profile at www.musicuganda.com/chameleone.html (accessed September 11, 2007).

7. "Accra Reclaims Hip-Hop," BBC World Service, November 4, 2003, 1, available at www.news.bbc.co.uk/2/hi/africa/3241007.stm (accessed April 9, 2004).

8. "African Hip Hop Warriors: Interview with Yumus Rafiq," africanhiphop.com, January 15, 2005, available at www.africanhiphop.com/index.php?module=subjects&func=viewpage&pageid=227 (accessed September 23, 2006).

9. This practice was popularized by Congolese musicians who migrated to East Africa during political turmoil in their country.

10. Actually, this song is very similar in structure and text to American rapper Redman's song "What You Lookin' 4?" in the album *Muddy Waters;* part of the chorus is

"I said what the ——— are you lookin' 4? Can't a young man make money anymore?" And Gidi Gidi and Maji Maji say, "Who the hell are you looking for? Can't a young Luo make money anymore?" The song is also similar to Murda Mase's song "Lookin' at Me": "Now what the hell is you lookin' for? / Can't a young man get money anymore? / Let my pants sag down to the floor."

11. This is the hit song from the album *Machozi, Jasho, na Damu* (Tears, sweat, and blood) produced in 2001.

12. The interview is available at www.youtube.com/watch?v=owmxj7sCvoE (accessed September 30, 2007).

13. Malcolm X, "Message to the Grassroots," November 10, 1963, Top 100 Speeches, American Rhetoric, available at www.americanrhetoric.com/speeches/malcolmxgrassroots.htm (accessed February 12, 2006).

14. Their song "Hitaji (Need)" proves this point even through the entire song is choreographed and sung in a very clear Western style.

3. Move Over, Boys, the Girls Are Here: Hip Hop and Gendered Identities

1. Thus far, only Mwangi (2004) and Perullo (2005) have addressed gender and hip hop as an analytical category and important discursive practice, respectively, in East Africa. Mwangi takes on an analysis of East African hip hop through a prism of masculinity and argues that many artists position their construction of nationalism on masculinized memory; while Perullo cites the work of Mr. II and later Zay B as important commentators of the plight of women in Tanzania.

2. In January 2004, the *Daily Nation* ran stories of female university students who were engaging in commercial sex to sustain themselves through school while others turned to hawking to raise funds to finance their college education. Such vulnerable youth will quickly fall prey to men with disposable income who lure them with material things for their sexual pleasure and later abandon them.

3. See Alakok Mayombo, "Children Drawn into Sex Trade," InterPress Third World News Agency, April 27, 1998, available at www.hartford-hwp.com/archives/36/052.html (accessed September 3, 2005).

4. According to reports found on www.nationmaster.com, 50 percent, 36 percent, and 35 percent of Kenyans, Tanzanians, and Ugandans, respectively, live below the poverty line. This information is collated from reports from United Nations Development Programme (UNDP), *CIA World Factbook,* and the World Bank. On February 28, 2007, Kenya's lead daily newspaper, the *Daily Nation,* confirmed these data for Kenya showing that in 2005, 50 percent of Kenyans lived below the poverty line.

4. Economic Change and Political Deception

1. Professor Jay, personal communication, June 23, 2006, Dar es Salaam, Tanzania.

2. Ibid.

3. Ibid.

4. Central Intelligence Agency, "Kenya," *World Factbook,* May 23, 2007, available at https://www.cia.gov/library/publications/the-world-factbook/geos/ke.html (accessed May 23, 2007).

5. "Strategic Framework, 2007/08," Makerere University, April 2, 2007, available at www.makerere.ac.ug/makict/documents/strategic_framework/chap3.html (accessed August 13, 2007).

6. Richard Wanambwa, "Sex for Marks at Makerere" *Daily Monitor,* July 28, 2007, available at http://allafrica.com/stories/200707270882.html (accessed August 14, 2007).

7. Ken Ouko, "Kenyan Tutor on 'Sex for Grades,'" BBC News, May 2, 2007, available at http://news.bbc.co.uk/1/hi/world/africa/6612681.stm (accessed August 14, 2007).

8. For examples of such practices in Zambia, visit www.un-ngls.org, and in Ivory Coast, visit www.ban.org. These two sites were accessed January 31, 2007.

5. Morality, Health, and the Politics of Sexuality in an Era of HIV/AIDS

1. *Daily Nation,* July 17, 2004, 22.

2. For more information on these organizations and their various programs, see www.twaweza.org, www.chezasalama.com, and www.straight-talk.or.ug.

3. Philip Mwaniki, "Controversial Juala," *Daily Nation,* July 4, 2004, 3.

4. "Blessed Land of Cardinals," *East African,* April 11, 2005, available at www.nationmedia.com/eastafrican/ (accessed July 31, 2007).

5. I have limited myself to heterosexual relations throughout this work.

6. Jane Godia, "Women Unable to Negotiate for Safe Sex," *East African Standard,* July 1, 2007, Standard Group, available at http://www.eastandard.net/archives/InsidePage.php?&id=1143970662&catid=159&a=1 (accessed July 13, 2007).

7. "Tanzanian Anglican Church Still Opposes Condoms, Sex Education," *Guardian,* August 12, 2006, IPP Media, available at www.ippmedia.com/ipp/guardian/2006/08/12/72269.html (accessed July 31, 2007).

8. "Uganda: Back Condom Use, Museveni Urges Catholic Leaders," Humanitarian News and Analysis, June 15, 2005, available at http://www.irinnews.org/Report.aspx?reportid=38692 (accessed July 31, 2007).

9. See Joyce Mulama, "Commonwealth Event Debates Why AIDS Wears 'the Face of a Woman,'" June 14, 2007, available at www.ipsnews.net/africa/nota.asp?idnews=38172 (accessed August 5, 2007).

10. Leigh Shafer, quoted in Michael Marco and Edwin J. Bernard, "Is Uganda's HIV Prevention Success Story 'Unravelling'?" available at www.aidsmap.com/en/news/E7A3F648–945A-405D-BF00–89BA7E7FDCDF.asp (accessed August 3, 2007),

11. Professor Jay, interview by author, June 23, 2006, Dar es Salaam, Tanzania.

12. Ferooz Mrisho, interview, *Kenya Times*, October 24, 2006, available at www
.timesnews.co.ke/24oct06/spicy/spicy8.html (accessed August 27, 2007).

13. Ibid.

6. Staying True to the Cause: Hip Hop's Enduring Social Role

1. "Up-close with Jose Chameleone," interview by Steve Tendo, www.musicuganda
.com, January 20, 2005, available at http://www.musicuganda.com/chameleone.html
(accessed September 10, 2007).

2. "History," Ukooflani Mau Mau, Ukooflani Official Site, October 22, 2006, available
at www.ukooflanimaumau.com/site/en/history.html (accessed January 23, 2007).

References

"Accra Reclaims Hip-Hop." BBC World Service, November 4, 2003. www.news.bbc
.co.uk/2/hi/africa/3241007.stm (accessed April 9, 2004).

Achebe, Chinua. 1998. "Africa Is People." Presidential Fellow Lecture for the World Bank
Group, June 17, 1998. http://www.africaresource.com (accessed July 30, 2006).

Achieng, Judith. 1998. "Health: High Incidence of HIV in Kenya's Catholics, Official
Says." InterPress News Service (IPS) June 17, 1998. http://www.aegis.com/news/
ips/1998/IP980604.html (accessed August 20, 2007).

"African Hip Hop Warriors: Interview with Yumus Rafiq." africanhiphop.com, January
15, 2005. www.africanhiphop.com/index.php?module=subjects&func=viewpage&
pageid=227 (accessed September 23, 2006).

Ahmad, Khabir. 2001. "Namibian Government to Prosecute Healers." *Lancet* 357
(9253): 371.

Aina, Tade Akin, ed. 2004. *Globalisation and Social Policy in Africa*. Dakar, Senegal:
CODESRIA.

Ajayi, Ibi. 2001. "What Africa Needs to Do to Benefit from Globalization." *Finance
and Development: A Quarterly Magazine of the IMF* 38 (4). http://www.imf.org/
external/pubs/ft/andd/2001/12/ajayi.htm (accessed November 20, 2007).

Aké, Claude. 1982. *Social Science as Imperialism: The Theory of Political Development*.
Ibadan, Nigeria: Ibadan University Press.

Amadiume, Ifi. 1997. *Re-Inventing Africa: Matriarchy, Religion, and Culture*. London:
Zed.

Amin, Samir. 1998. *Capitalism in the Age of Globalization*. London: Zed.

Amselle, Jean-Loup. 2002. "Globalization and the Future of Anthropology." *African
Affairs* 101:213–29.

Anderson, David. 2002. "Vigilantes, Violence, and Politics of Public Order in Kenya."
African Affairs 101:531–55.

Anderson, Elijah. 1990. *Streetwise: Race, Class, and Change in an Urban Community.* Chicago: University of Chicago Press.

Androutsopoulos, Jannis, and Arno Scholz. 2003. "Spaghetti Funk: Appropriation of Hip-Hop Culture and Rap Music in Europe." *Popular Music and Society* 2:45–57.

Ani, Marimba. 1994. *Yurugu: An African-centered Critique of European Cultural Thought and Behavior.* Trenton, N.J.: Africa World.

Appadurai, Arjun. 1996. *Modernity at Large: Cultural Dimensions of Globalization.* Minneapolis: University of Minnesota Press.

Appiah, Anthony. 1993. *In My Father's House: Africa in the Philosophy of Culture.* London: Oxford University Press.

———. 1998. "Race, Pluralism, and Afrocentricity." *Journal of Blacks in Higher Education* 19:116–18.

Asante, Molefi. 1988. *Afrocentricity.* Trenton, N.J.: Africa World.

Askew, Kelly. 2002. *Performing the Nation: Swahili Music and Cultural Politics in Tanzania.* Chicago: University of Chicago Press.

Assefa, Taye, Severine Rugumamu, and Ahmed Gaffar, eds. 2002. *Globalization, Democracy and Development in Africa: Challenges and Prospects.* Addis Ababa, Ethiopia: OSSREA.

Auvert, Bertran, et al. 2001. "HIV Infection among Youth in a South African Mining Town Is Associated with Herpes Simplex Virus-2 Seropositivity and Sexual Behaviour." *AIDS: Journal of the International AIDS Society* 15 (7): 885–98.

Badsha, Farzanah. "Old Skool Rules/New Skool Breaks: Negotiating Identities in the Cape Town Hip-Hop Scene." In Wasserman and Jacobs 2003, 120–45.

Barkan, Joel. 2004. "Kenya after Moi." *Foreign Affairs* 83 (1): 1–6.

Barrett, Leonard. 1974. *Soul-Force: African Heritage in Afro-American Religion.* Garden City, N.Y.: Doubleday.

Barz, Gregory. 2001. "Meaning in Benga Music of Western Kenya. " *British Journal of Ethnomusicology* 10 (1): 107–15.

———. 2004. *Music in East Africa: Experiencing Music, Expressing Culture.* London: Oxford University Press.

Bascom, William, and Allan Dundes. 1994. *African Folktales in the New World.* Bloomington: Indiana University Press.

Basu, Dupannita, and Sidney Lemelle, eds. 2006. *The Vinyl Ain't Final: Hip Hop and the Globalization of Black Popular Culture.* London: Pluto.

Bates, Robert, Valentin Y. Mudimbe, and Jean O'Barr, eds. 1993. *Africa and the Disciplines: The Contributions of Research in Africa to the Social Sciences and Humanities.* Chicago: University of Chicago Press.

Battersby, Jane. "'Sometimes It Feels like I Am Not Black Enough'": Recast(e)ing Coloured through South African Hip-Hop as Post-colonial Text." In Wasserman and Jacobs 2003, 109–19.

Bayart, Jean-Francois. 1993. *The State in Africa: The Politics of the Belly.* New York: Longman.

Bayart, Jean-Francois, Stephen Ellis, and Béatrice Hibou. 1999. *The Criminalization of the State in Africa*. Bloomington: Indiana University Press.

Beck, Ulrich. 2000. *What Is Globalisation?* Trans. Patrick Camiller. New York: Blackwell.

Behar, Ruth, and Deborah Gordon, eds. 1995. *Women Writing Culture*. Berkeley: University of California Press.

Bennett, Andy. 1999. "Hip Hop am Main: The Localization of Rap Music and Hip Hop Culture." *Media, Culture, and Society* 21 (1): 71–91.

Bernal, Martin. 1987. *Black Athena: The Afroasiatic Roots of Classical Civilization*. London: Free Association.

Bernstein, Ann. 2002. "Globalization Culture and Development." In *Many Globalizations*, ed. Peter Berger and Samuel Huntington, 185–250. Oxford, U.K: Oxford University Press.

Best, Steven, and Douglas Kellner. 1999. "Rap, Black Rage, and Racial Difference." *Enculturation* 2 (2). http://enculturation.gmu.edu/2_2/best-kellner.html (accessed March 2, 2006).

Biersteker, Thomas. 1990. "Reducing the Role of the State in the Economy: A Conceptual Exploration of IMF and World Bank Prescriptions." *International Studies Quarterly* 34 (4): 477–92.

"Biographies—Chiz n Brain." Ukooflani Mau Mau, 2007. http://www.ukooflanimaumau .com/site/en/home/chizn_brain.html (accessed January 26, 2007).

Black, Jan Knippers. 1999. *Inequity in the Global Village : Recycled Rhetoric and Disposable People*. West Hartford, Conn.: Kumarian.

"Blessed Land of Cardinals." *East African*, April 11, 2005. www.nationmedia.com/ eastafrican/ (accessed July 31, 2007).

Bongmba, Elias. 2004. "Reflections on Thabo Mbeki's African Renaissance." *Journal of South African Studies* 30 (2): 291–316.

Bourgault, Louise. 1995. *Mass Media in Sub-Saharan Africa*. Bloomington: University of Indiana Press.

Bourgois, Philippe. 2002. *In Search of Respect: Selling Crack in El Barrio*. New York: Cambridge University Press.

Brecher, Jeremy, and Tim Costello. 1998. *Global Village or Global Pillage: Economic Reconstruction from the Bottom Up*. 2nd ed. Cambridge, Mass.: South End.

Brett, Edwin Allan. 1973. *Colonialism and Underdevelopment in East Africa: The Politics of Economic Change, 1919–1939*. Oxford, U.K.: Heinemann.

Brubaker, Rogers, and Fredrick Cooper. 2000. "Beyond 'Identity.'" *Theory and Society* 29 (1): 1–47.

Bruner, Edward. 2005. *Culture on Tour: Ethnographies of Travel*. Chicago: University of Chicago Press.

Bryceson, Deborah. 2000. "Of Criminals and Clients: African Culture and Afro-Pessimism in a Globalized World." *Canadian Journal of African Studies* 34 (2): 417–42.

Burgess, Thomas. 2005. "Introduction to Youth and Citizenship in East Africa." *Africa Today* 51 (3): vii–xxiv.

Butler, Judith. 1990. *Gender Trouble: Feminism and the Subversion of Identity.* London: Routledge.

Callaghy, Thomas, and John Ravenhill. 1994. "Vision, Politics, and Structure: Afro-Optimism, Afro-Pessimism, or Reality?" In *Hemmed In: Responses to Africa's Economic Decline,* ed. Callaghy and Ravenhill, 1–17. New York: Columbia University Press.

Carovano, Kathryn. 1992. "More Than Mothers and Whores: Redefining the AIDS Prevention Needs of Women." *International Journal of Health Services* 21 (1): 131–42.

Carpenter, L. M., A. Kamali, A. Ruberantwari, S. S. Malamba, and J. A. Whitworth. 1999. "Rates of HIV-1 Transmission within Marriage in Rural Uganda in Relation to the HIV Sero-status of the Partners." *AIDS* 13 (9): 1083–89.

Casco, Jose Arturo Saveedra. 2006. "The Language of Young People: Rap, Urban Culture, and Protest in Tanzania." *Journal of Asian and African Studies* 41 (3): 229–48.

Catholic Secretariat Commission for Health. 2006. "This We Teach and Do." Kenya Episcopal Conference. http://www.kec.or.ke/viewdocument.asp?ID=19 (accessed July 31, 2007).

Central Intelligence Agency. "Kenya." *World Factbook.* https://www.cia.gov/library/publications/the-world-factbook/geos/ke.html (accessed May 23, 2007).

Chabal, Patrick. 2002. "The Quest for Good Governance and Development in Africa: Is NEPAD the Answer?" *International Affairs* 78 (3): 447–62.

Chalfin, Brenda. 2000. "Risky Business: Economic Uncertainty, Market Reforms and Female Livelihoods in Northeast Ghana." *Development and Change* 31:987–1008.

Cheru, Fantu. 2002. *African Renaissance: Roadmaps to the Challenge of Globalization.* London: Zed.

Clark, Shelley. 2004. "Early Marriage and HIV Risks in Sub-Saharan Africa." *Studies in Family Planning* 35 (3): 149–60.

Collins, John. 1976. "Ghanaian Highlife." *African Arts* 10 (1): 62–68.

Comaroff, John, and Jean Comaroff. 1991. *Of Revelation and Revolution: Christianity, Colonialism, and Consciousness in South Africa.* Chicago: University of Chicago Press.

———. 1992. *Ethnography and the Historical Imagination.* Boulder, Colo.: Westview.

Condry, Ian. 2006. *Hip Hop Japan: Rap and the Paths of Cultural Globalization.* Durham, N.C.: Duke University Press.

Conyers, James, ed. 1997. *African Studies: A Disciplinary Quest for Both Theory and Method.* Jefferson, N.C.: McFarland.

Cooper, Fredrick. 2001. "What Is the Concept of Globalization Good For? An African Historian's Perspective." *African Affairs* 100 (399): 189–213.

Crowder, Michael. 1987a. "'Us' and 'Them': The International African Institute and the Current Crisis of Identity in African Studies. *Africa* 57 (1): 109–22.

———. 1987b. "Whose Dream Was It Anyway? Twenty-five Years of African Independence." *African Affairs* 86 (342): 7–24.

Dimitriadis, Greg. 1996. "From Live Performance to Mediated Narrative." *Popular Music* 15 (2): 179–94.

Diop, Cheikh Anta. 1974. *African Origins of Civilization: Myth of Reality.* Trans. Mercer Cook. Chicago: Hill.

Diouf, Mamadou. 2003. "Engaging Postcolonial Cultures: African Youth and Public Space." *African Studies Review* 49 (1): 1–12.

DjeDje, Jacqueline Cogdell, ed. 1999. *Turn Up the Volume! A Celebration of African Music.* Los Angeles: UCLA Fowler Museum of Cultural History.

Dolby, Nadine. 2006. "Popular Culture and Public Space in Africa: The Possibilities of Cultural Citizenship." *African Studies Review* 49 (3): 31–47.

Durham, Deborah. 2000. "Youth and the Social Imagination in Africa: Introduction to Parts 1 and 2." *Anthropological Quarterly* 73 (3): 113–20.

Edelman, Marc, and Angelique Haugerud, eds. 2005. *The Anthropology of Development and Globalization.* Malden, Mass.: Blackwell.

———. "Introduction: The Anthropology of Development and Globalization." In Edelman and Haugerud 2005, 1–74.

Epprecht, Marc. 2003. "Why I Love African Studies." *African Studies Quarterly* 7 (2 and 3). http://web.africa.ufl.edu/asq/v7/v7i2a16.htm (accessed July 14, 2006).

Fabian, Johannes. 1978. "Popular Culture in Africa: Findings and Conjunctures." *Africa* 48 (4): 315–34.

Fardon, Richard, Wim van Binsbergen, and Rijk Van Dijk, eds. 1994. *Modernity on a Shoestring: Dimensions of Globalization, Consumption, and Development in Africa and Beyond.* Leiden, The Netherlands: EIDOS.

Fenn, John B. 2004. "Rap and Ragga Musical Cultures, Lifestyles, and Performances in Malawi." PhD diss., Indiana University.

Fenn, John B., and Alex Perullo. 2000. "Language Choices and Hip Hop in Tanzania and Malawi." *Popular Music and Society* 24 (3): 73–90.

Ferguson, James. 1998. *Expectations of Modernity: Myths and Meanings of Urban Life on the Zambian Copperbelt.* Berkeley: University of California Press.

———. 2005. "Seeing like an Oil Company: Space, Security, and Global Capital in Neoliberal Africa." *America Anthropologist* 107 (3): 377–82.

———. 2006. *Global Shadows: Africa in the Neoliberal World Order.* Durham, N.C.: Duke University Press.

Ferrari, Aurelia. 2007. "Hip Hop in Nairobi: Recognition of an International Movement and the Main Means of Expression for the Urban Youth in Poor Residential Areas." In wa Njogu and Mapeau 2007, 107–28.

Flynn, Karen. 2005. *Food, Culture, and Survival in an African City.* New York: Palgrave Macmillan.

Forman, Murray. 2002. "Keeping It Real? African Identities and Hip Hop." In *Music, Popular Culture, Identities,* ed. Richard Young, 34–89. Amsterdam: Rodopi.

Friedman, Jonathan. 2005. "Globalization, Dis-Integration, Re-Organization: The Transformations of Violence." In Edelman and Haugerud 2005, 160–68.

Geertz, Clifford. 1973. *Interpretation of Cultures*. New York: Basic Books.

Giddens, Anthony. 2003. *Runaway World: How Globalization Is Reshaping Our Lives*. New York: Routledge.

Gilroy, Paul. 1992. *The Black Atlantic: Modernity and Double Consciousness*. Cambridge, Mass.: Harvard University Press.

Godia, Jane. "Women Unable to Negotiate for Safe Sex." *East African Standard*, July 1, 2007, Standard Group. http://www.eastandard.net/archives/InsidePage.php?&id=1143970662&catid=159&a=1 (accessed July 13, 2007).

Gottlieb, Alma, and Philip Graham. 1994. *Parallel Worlds: An Anthropologist and Writer Encounter Africa*. Chicago: University of Chicago Press.

———. 1999. "Revising the Text, Revisioning the Field: Reciprocity over the Long Term." *Anthropology and Humanism* 24 (2): 117–28.

Government of Kenya. 2003. "Economic Recovery Strategy for Wealth and Employment." Ministry of Planning and National Development, June 2, 2003. www.monitoring.go.ke/images/stories/publications/economic_recovery_plan.pdf (accessed December 27, 2007).

Green, Elliott. 2005. "Ethnicity and the Politics of Land Tenure Reform in Central Uganda." Working Paper 05-58. Institute of Development Studies, London School of Economics.

Gunderson, Frank, and Gregory Barz, eds. *Mashindano! Competitive Music Performance in East Africa*. Dar es Salaam, Tanzania: Mkuki na Nyota.

Gupta, Akhil. 1998. *Postcolonial Developments: Agriculture in the Making of Modern India*. Durham, N.C.: Duke University Press.

Gupta, Geeta Rao. 2000. "Gender, Sexuality, and HIV/AIDS: The What, the Why, and the How." Plenary Address at the thirteenth International AIDS Conference, Durban, South Africa, July 12, 2000. www.icrw.org/docs/Durban_HIVAIDS_speech700.pdf (accessed July 20, 2007).

Gyekye, Kwame. 1997. *Tradition and Modernity: Philosophical Reflections on the African Experience*. New York: Oxford University Press.

Haas, Peter Jan, and Thomas Gesthuizen. 2000. "Ndani ya Bongo: Kiswahili Rap Keeping It Real." In Gunderson and Barz 2000, 279–94.

"Hali Halisi Rap as an Alternative Medium." africanhiphop.com, November 10, 2004. www.africanhiphop.com/index.php?module=subjects&func=viewpage&pageid=220 (accessed January 21, 2006).

Hansen, Karen Tranberg. 2000. *Salaula: The World of Secondhand Clothing and Zambia*. Chicago: University of Chicago Press.

Harris, Richard, and Melinda Seid, eds. 2000. *Critical Perspectives on Globalization and Neoliberalism in the Developing Countries*. Boston: Brill.

Harvey, David. 2000. *Spaces of Hope*. Berkeley: University of California Press.

Hasty, Jennifer. 2005. "The Pleasure of Corruption: Desire and Discipline in Ghanaian Political Culture." *Cultural Anthropology* 20 (2): 271–301.

Haugerud, Angelique. 1995. *The Culture of Politics in Modern Kenya*. Cambridge: Cambridge University Press.

Haupt, Adam. 2001. "Black Thing: Hip-Hop Nationalism, 'Race', and Gender in Prophets of da City and Brasse vannie Kaap." In *Coloured by History Shaped by Place: New Perspectives on Coloured Identities in Cape Town*, ed. Zimitri Erasmus, 121–34. Cape Town, South Africa: Kwela.

Hazzard-Donald, Katrina. 2004. "Dance in Hip Hop Culture." In *Hip-hop Studies Reader*, ed. Forman Murray and Mark Anthony Neal, 505–16. New York: Routledge.

Held, David, and Anthony McGrew, eds. 2000. *The Global Transformations Reader: An Introduction to the Globalization Debate*. Cambridge, U.K.: Polity.

Hirst, Paul, and Graham Thompson. 1999. *Globalization in Question*. 2nd ed. Cambridge, U.K.: Polity.

Hofmeyr, Isabel, Joyce Nyairo, and James Ogude. 2003. "'Who Can Bwogo Me?' Popular Culture in Kenya." *Social Identities* 9 (3): 373–82.

Human Rights Watch. 1997. *Juvenile Injustice, Police Abuse, and Detention of Street Children in Kenya*. New York: Human Rights Watch.

Hunter-Gault, Charlyne. 2007. *New News from Africa: Uncovering Africa's Renaissance*. London: Oxford University Press.

Hyders, Goran. 1996. "African Studies in the Mid-1990s: Between Afro-Pessimism and Amero-Skepticism." *African Studies Review* 39 (2): 1–17.

Impey, Angela. 2001. "Resurrecting the Flesh? Reflections on Women in Kwaito." *Agenda* 49:45.

Isbister, John. 2006. *Promises Not Kept: Poverty and the Betrayal of Third World Development*. Sterling, Va.: Kumarian.

Jewsiewicki, Bogumil. 2006. "Postscriptural Communication, Postphotographic Images, Performance as Heritage Preservation: Invention as Tradition in Africa." Association of Africanist Anthropology Distinguished Lecture, San Jose, California. November 16, 2006.

Jones, Barry. 1995. *Globalization and Interdependence in the International Political Economy*. London: Frances International.

Joseph, Richard. 1998. "Africa, 1990–1997: From Abertura to Closure." *Journal of Democracy* 9 (2): 3–17.

———. 2003. "Africa: States in Crisis." *Journal of Democracy* 14 (3): 159–70.

Kabwegyere, Tarsis B. 1974. *The Politics of State Formation: The Nature and Effects of Colonialism in Uganda*. Nairobi, Kenya: East African Literature Bureau.

Kagwanja, Peter Mwangi. 2005. "'Power to Uhuru': Youth Identity and Generational Politics in Kenya's 2002 Elections." *African Affairs* 105 (418): 51–75.

Kalyvas, Stathis. 2003. "The Ontology of Political Violence: Action and Identity in Civil Wars." *American Political Science Review* 1 (3): 475–94.

Kangara, Lucy. 2005. "The Church, Youth, and Sexuality in Kenya." *Sexuality in Africa Magazine* 2 (2): 8–10.

Kaniki, Martin, ed. 1980. *Tanzania under Colonial Rule*. London: Longman.

Kanyinga, Karuti. 1997. "The Land Question and Politics of Tenure in Kenya." *IDR Currents* 15:17–20.

Kariuki, John, Amos Ngaira, Moses Serugo, Evelyn Matsamura, and David Macky. 2004. "Without Tom Mboya, Makeba Wouldn't Have Sung Malaika." *Monitor,* March 15, 2004.

Katumanga, Musambayi. 2007. "Folk Poetry as a Weapon of Struggle: An Analysis of Chaka Mchaka Resistance Songs of the National Resistance Movement/Army of Uganda." In wa Njogu and Mapeau 2007, 129–56.

Kearney, Michael. 1995. "The Local and the Global: The Anthropology of Globalization and Transnationalism." *Annual Review of Anthropology* 24:547–65.

Kelley, Robin. 2006. Foreword to Basu and Lemelle 2006, i–x.

Kidula, Jean. 2000. "The Impact of the Christian Music Industry in Shaping Theological and Musical Trends in Kenya." *Worship Leader* 43 (1): 4–11.

———. 2006. "Ethnomusicology, the Music Canon, and African Music: Positions, Tensions, and Resolutions in the African Academy." *Africa Today* 52 (3): 99–113.

Korang, Kwaku. 2003. *Writing Ghana, Imagining Africa: Nation and African Modernity.* Rochester, N.Y.: University of Rochester Press.

Kubik, Gerhard. 1999. *Africa and the Blues.* Jackson: University Press of Mississippi.

Kunzler, Daniel. 2006. "Hip Hop Movements in Mali and Burkina Faso: The Local Adaptation of a Global Culture." Paper, sixteenth International Sociological Association World Congress of Sociology. Durban, South Africa.

Larkin, Brian. 2004. "Degraded Images, Distorted Sounds: Nigerian Video and the Infrastructure of Piracy." *Public Culture* 16 (2): 289–314.

Leggett, Tedd, Valerie Moller, and Robbin Richards. 1997. *My Life in the New South Africa: A Youth Perspective.* Pretoria, South Africa: Human Science Research Council.

Lemelle, Sidney. 2006. "'Ni Wapi Tunakwenda': Hip Hop Culture and the Children of Arusha." In Basu and Lemelle 2006, 209–34.

Lewellen, Ted. 2002. *The Anthropology of Globalization: Cultural Anthropology Enters the 21st Century.* Westport, Conn.: Greenwood.

Leys, Colin. 1980. *Underdevelopment in Kenya: The Political Economy of Neo-Colonialism, 1964–71.* London: Currey.

Lonsdale, John, and Bruce Berman. 1979. "Coping with the Contradictions: The Development of the Colonial State in Kenya, 1895–1914." *Journal of African History* 20 (4): 487–505.

Lull, James. 1995. *Media, Communication, Culture: A Global Approach.* Cambridge, U.K.: Polity.

Macamo, Elisio Salvado, ed. 2005. *Negotiating Modernity: Africa's Ambivalent Experience.* London: Zed.

Mafeje, Archie. 2000. "Africanity: Combative Ontology." *Codesria Bulletin* 1:66–71.

———. 2001. "Africanity: A Commentary by Way of Conclusion." *Codesria Bulletin* 3 and 4:17–19.

Magubane, Zine. 2006. "Globalization and Gangster Rap: Hip Hop in the Post-Apartheid City." In Basu and Lemelle 2006, 207–27.

Malcolm X. "Message to the Grassroots." November 10, 1963. Top 100 Speeches, American Rhetoric. www.americanrhetoric.com/speeches/malcolmxgrassroots .htm (accessed February 12, 2006).

Malekela, George A. 1991. "Educated Youth Unemployment in Tanzania." In Social Problems in Eastern Africa, ed. C. K. Omari and L. P. Shaidi, 40–54. Dar es Salaam, Tanzania: Dar es Salaam University Press.

Mama, Amina. 2002. "Challenging Subjects: Gender and Power in African Contexts." In Identity and Beyond: Rethinking Africanity, discussion paper 12, 9–17. Uppsala, Sweden: Nordic African Institute.

Mama, Amina, Ayesha Imam, and Fatou Sow, eds. 1997. Engendering African Social Sciences. Dakar: CODESRIA.

Maman, Suzanne, et al. 2000. "History of Partner Violence Is Common among Women Attending a Voluntary Counselling and Testing Clinic in Dar es Salaam, Tanzania." Paper presented at the thirteenth International AIDS Conference. Durban, South Africa. July 9–14, 2000.

Mamdani, Mahmood. 1996. Citizen and Subject: Contemporary Africa and the Legacy of Colonialism. Princeton, N.J.: Princeton University Press.

Mwaniki, Philip. "Controversial Juala." Daily Nation, July 4, 2004.x

Marco, Michael, and Edwin J. Bernard. 2007 August 3. "Is Uganda's HIV Prevention Success Story 'Unravelling'?" aidsmap, August 22, 2006. www.aidsmap.com/en/news/ E7A3F648-945A-405D-BF00-89BA7E7FDCDF.asp (accessed August 3, 2007).

Masolo, David. 2000. "Presencing the Past and Remembering the Present: Social Features of Popular Music in Kenya." In Music and Radical Imagination, ed. Ronald Rodano and Philip Bohlman, 349–402. Chicago: University of Chicago Press.

Masuguliko, Renatus. 2007. "Wambonda Mwalimu Mzinzi." Nipashe, April 14, 2007. www.ippmedia.com/ipp/nipashe/2007/04/14/88405.html (accessed August 21, 2007).

Mayer, Ruth. 2002. Artificial Africas: Colonial Images in the Times of Globalization. Hanover, N.H.: University Press of New England.

Mbembe, Achille. 2002. "African Modes of Self-Writing." Public Culture 14 (1): 239–73.

Mbugua, Njeri. 2007. "Factors Inhibiting Educated Mothers in Kenya from Giving Meaningful Sex-Education to their Daughters." Social Science and Medicine 64:1079–89.

McFadden, Patricia. 2001. "Political Power: the Challenges of Sexuality, Patriarchy, and Globalisation in Africa." Paper delivered at a seminar hosted by the Mauritius Women's Movement (MLF) and the Workers Education Association (LPT). Port Louis, Mauritius, February 12–17, 2001.

Mengara, Daniel, ed. 2001. Images of Africa: Stereotypes and Realities. Trenton, N.J.: Africa World.

Millennium Campaign. 2006. "African Youth Set Agenda for World Social Forum." www.milleniumcampaign.org (accessed December 13, 2006).

Miller, Christopher. 1990. *Theories of Africans: Francophone Literature and Anthropology in Africa.* Chicago: University of Chicago Press.

Miller, Daniel. 1997. *Capitalism: An Ethnographic Approach.* Oxford: Berg.

Miller, Toby. 1998. *Technologies of Truth: Cultural Citizenship and the Popular Media.* Minneapolis: University of Minneapolis Press.

Mitchell, Tony. 2002. "Introduction: Another Root—Hip-Hop Outside of the USA." In *Global Noise: Rap and Hip-Hop Outside the USA,* ed. Mitchell, 1–38. Middleton, Conn.: Wesleyan University Press.

Mkandawire, Thandika. 1994. "Adjustment, Political Conditionality and Democratisation in Africa." In *From Adjustment to Development in Africa: Conflict, Controversy, Convergence, Consensus,* ed. Giovanni Andrea Cornia and Gerald K. Helleiner, 89–108. London: Palgrave Macmillan.

———. 2002. "Globalisation, Equity, and Social Development." *African Sociological Review* 6 (1): 1–18. http://www.codesria.org/Links/Publications/asr6_1full/thandika.pdf (accessed September 22, 2006).

Mkandawire, Thandika, and Charles Soludo. 1999. *Our Continent Our Future: African Perspective on Structural Adjustments.* Trenton, N.J.: Africa World.

Mohanty, Chandra, Ann Russo, and Lourdes Torres, eds. 1991. *Third World Women and the Politics of Feminism.* Bloomington: Indiana University Press.

Moyer, Eileen. 2005. "Street-Corner Justice in the Name of Jah: Imperatives for Peace among Dar es Salaam Street Youth." *Africa Today* 51:31–58.

Mphande, Lupenga, and Ikechukwu Okafor Newsum. 1997. "Popular Music, Appropriation, and the Circular Culture of Labor Migration in Southern Africa: The Case of South Africa and Malawi." In *Language, Rhythm, and Sound: Black Popular Cultures into the Twenty-first Century,* ed. J. Adjaye and Adrienne Andrews, 88–112. Pittsburgh, Penn.: University of Pittsburgh Press.

Mudimbe, Valentin Y. 1988. *The Invention of Africa: Gnosis, Philosophy, and the Order of Knowledge.* Bloomington: Indiana University Press.

Muendo, Stevens, and Tony Mochama. 2007. "Regional Collabos the Way to Go." *Pulse Magazine.* www.estandard.net/mag/mag.php?id=1143978185&catid=123 (accessed December 7, 2007).

Muller, Jean-Claude. 1975. "Clan Headship and Political Change among the Rukuba (Benue-Plateau State, Nigeria)." *Canadian Journal of African Studies* 9 (1): 3–16

Murunga, Godwin, and Shadrack Nasong'o. 2007. *Kenya: The Struggle for Democracy.* London: Zed.

Mutahaba, Gelase, and Kithinji Kiragu. 2002. "Lesson of International and African Perspectives on Public Service Reform: Examples from Five African Nations." *Africa Development* 27 (3 and 4):48–75.

Mutonya, Maina. 2005. "Mugithi Performance: Popular Music, Stereotypes, and Ethnic Identity." *Africa Insight* 35 (2): 53–60.

Mwangi, Evan. 2004. "Masculinity and Nationalism in East African Hip Hop Music." *Tydskrif vir Letterkunde* 4 (2): 5–20.

Mwenda, Andrew. 2006. "Taking Time to Contemplate." *Daily Monitor,* August 18, 2006.

Nannyonga-Tamusuza, Sylvia. 2002. "Gender, Ethnicity, and Politics in Kadongo-Kamu Music of Uganda: Analysing the Song Kayanda." In *Playing with Identities in Contemporary Music in Africa,* ed. M. Palmberg and A. Kirkegaard, 143–48. Uppsala, Sweden: Nordiska Afrikainstitutet.

Nazer, Hisham. 1999. *Power of a Third Kind: the Western Attempt to Colonize the Global Village.* Westport, Conn.: Praeger.

"New Music Exiles Settle in Nairobi." Special report. *Daily Nation,* March 17, 2004.

Ngesa, Mildred. 2007. "Setback for Anti-AIDS Fight as Patients Sell Drugs to Buy Food." *Daily Nation,* March 17, 2007.

Nolan, Riall W. 1999. *Communicating and Adapting across Cultures: Living and Working in the Global Village.* Westport, Conn.: Bergin and Garvey.

Ntarangwi, Mwenda. 1992. "Gender as Expressed through Verbal Art: Swahili Women Singers." Research report. Organization for Social Science Research in Eastern Africa. Addis Ababa, Ethiopia.

———. 1999. "Musical Performance as a Gender Experience: Examples from Kenya and Zimbabwe." In *Reflecting on Gender in Africa,* ed. Patricia McFadden, 27–54. Harare, Zimbabwe: Sapes.

———. 2000. "Malumbano or Matukano? Competition, Confrontation, and (De) Construction of Masculinity in the Taarab of Maulidi and Bhalo." In *Mashindano: Music and Competition in Eastern Africa,* ed. Gregory Barz and Frank Gunderson, 55–66. Dar es Salaam, Tanzania: Mkuki na Nyota.

———. 2003a. "The Challenges of Education and Development in Post-Colonial Kenya." *Africa Development* 28 (3 and 4):209–25.

———. 2003b. "Engendering Popular Music in East Africa: The Case of Taarab in Mombasa, Kenya." Paper presented at an international workshop, "Local Perspectives on the Local: Islam, Popular Culture, and Taarab in East Africa." University of Bayreuth, Germany, May 28–29, 2003.

———. 2003c. *Gender Identity and Performance: Understanding Swahili Social Realities through Song.* Trenton, N.J.: Africa World.

———. 2004. "Hip-Hop and Africanity in Global Perspective: Some Examples from East Africa." Paper presented at the fourteenth annual conference of the Pan African Anthropological Association. University of Ghana, Accra, Ghana, August 2–6, 2004.

———. 2006a. "From Nairobi to the Bronx: Hip Hop and the Politics of Africanity." Paper presented at the African Literature Association annual meeting. University of Ghana, Accra, Ghana, May 17–21, 2006.

———. 2006b. "Hip Hop and the Politics of Development in Kenya." Paper presented at the African Studies Association annual meeting. San Jose, Calif., November 19–22, 2006.

———. 2007. "Hip-Hop, Westernization, and Gender in East Africa." In wa Njogu and Mapeau 2007, 273–302.

Nyairo, Joyce. 2004. "'Reading the Referents': The Ghost of America in Contemporary Kenyan Popular Music." *Scrutiny* 29 (1): 39–45.

———. 2005a. "'Modify': Jua Kali as a Metaphor for Africa's Urban Ethnicities." Mary Kingsley Lecture, School of Oriental and African Studies (SOAS). Royal African Society, July 2, 2005. www.royalafricansociety.org (accessed October 12, 2006).

———. 2005b. "'Zilizopendwa': Kayamba Afrika's Use of Cover Versions, Remix and Sampling in the (Re)membering of Kenya." *African Studies* 64 (1): 29–54.

Nyairo, Joyce, and James Ogude. 2003. "Popular Music and the Negotiation of Contemporary Kenyan Identity: The Example of Nairobi City Ensemble." *Social Identities* 9 (3): 383–400.

———. 2005. "Popular Music, Popular Politics: Unbwogable and the Idioms of Freedom in Kenyan Popular Music." *African Affairs* 104 (415): 225–49.

Nyang'oro, Julius. 2002. "The Challenge of Development in Tanzania: The Legacy of Julius Nyerere." In *The Legacies of Julius Nyerere: Influences on Development Discourse and Practice in Africa,* ed. David McDonald and Eunice Njeri Sahle, 27–38. Trenton, N.J.: Africa World.

Nyerere, Julius. 1968. *Uhuru na Ujamaa: Freedom and Socialism.* Dar es Salaam, Tanzania: Oxford University Press.

Nzioka, Charles. 2004. "Unwanted Pregnancy and Sexually Transmitted Infection among Young Women in Rural Kenya." *Culture, Health, and Sexuality* 6 (1): 31–44

Obbo, Christine. 2006. "But We Know It All! African Perspectives on Anthropological Knowledge." In *African Anthropologies: History, Critique and Practice,* ed. Mwenda Ntarangwi, David Mills, and Mustafa Babiker, 254–76. Dakara, Senegal: CODESRIA.

Offiong, Daniel A. 2001. *Globalisation: Post Neo-Dependency and Poverty in Africa.* Lagos, Nigeria: Fourth Dimension.

Ogawa, Sayaka. 2006. "Earning among Friends: Business Practices and Creed among Petty Traders in Tanzania." *African Studies Quarterly* 9 (1 and 2). http://web.africa .ufl.edu/asq/v9/v9ia3.htm (accessed on January 23, 2007).

Ogot, Bethwell A. 1999. *Building on the Indigenous: Selected Essays, 1981–1998.* Kisumu, Kenya: Anyange.

Ogude, James. 2007. "'The Cat That Ate the Homestead Chicken': Murder, Memory, and Fabulization in D. O. Misiani's Dissident Music." In *Urban Legends, Colonial Myths: Popular Culture and Literature in East Africa,* ed. James Ogude and Joyce Nyairo, 173–203. Trenton, N.J.: Africa World.

Ohingo, Onyango. 2006. "Women, Youth Must Fight for Leadership." *East African Standard,* November 16, 2006.

Okpewho, Isidore, Carole Boyce Davies, and Ali A. Mazrui, eds. 2001. *The African Diaspora: African Origins and New World Identities.* Bloomington: Indiana University Press.

Olaniyan, Tejumola. 2004. *Arrest the Music! Fela and His Rebel Art and Politics*. Bloomington: Indiana University Press.

Olukoshi, Adebayo, and Francis Nyamnjoh. 2004. Editorial. *CODESRIA* 1 and 2:1–2.

Ong, Aihwa. 1999. *Flexible Citizenship: The Cultural Logics of Transnationality*. Durham, N.C.: Duke University Press.

———. 2006. *Neoliberalism as Exception: Mutations of Citizenship and Sovereignty*. Durham, N.C.: Duke University Press.

Ortner, Sherry. 2005. "Subjectivity and Cultural Critique." *Anthropological Theory* 5 (1): 31–52.

———. 2006. *Anthropology and Social Theory: Culture, Power and Acting Subject*. Durham, N.C.: Duke University Press.

Ouko, Ken. "Kenyan Tutor on 'Sex for Grades.'" BBC News, May 2, 2007. http://news .bbc.co.uk/1/hi/world/africa/6612681.stm (accessed August 14, 2007).

Palmberg, Mai, and Annemette Kirkegaard, eds. 2002. *Playing with Identities in Contemporary Music in Africa*. Uppsala, Sweden: Nordiska Afrikainstitutet.

Parikh, Shanti. 2004. "Sex, Lies and Love Letters: Condoms, Female Agency, and Paradoxes of Romance in Uganda." *Agenda: African Feminisms* 62 (2): 2–20.

———. 2005. "From Auntie to Disco: The Bifurcation of Risk and Pleasure in Sex Education in Uganda." In *Sex in Development: Science, Sexuality, and Morality in Global Perspective*, ed. V. Adams and S. L. Pigg, 125–58. Durham, N.C.: Duke University Press.

———. 2007. "The Political Economy of Marriage and HIV: The ABC Approach, the 'Safe' Infidelity, and Managing Moral Risk in Uganda." *American Journal of Public Health* 97 (7): 1198–208.

P'Bitek, Okot. 1970. *Western Religions in African Scholarship*. Nairobi, Kenya: East African.

———. 1984. *Song of Lawino and Song of Ocol*. Oxford, U.K.: Heinemann.

Pels, Peter. 1997. "The Anthropology of Colonialism: Culture, History, and the Emergence of Western Governmentality." *Annual Review of Anthropology* 26: 163–83.

Perry, Donna. 2000. "Rural Weekly Markets and the Dynamics of Time, Space, and Community in Senegal." *Journal of Modern African Studies* 38 (3): 461–86.

Perullo, Alex. 2005. "Hooligans and Heroes: Youth Identity and Hip-hop in Dar es Salaam, Tanzania." *Africa Today* 51:75–101.

———. 2007. "'Here's a Little Something Local': An Early History of Hip Hop in Dar es Salaam, Tanzania, 1984–1997." In *Dar es Salaam: The History of an Emerging East African Metropolis*, ed. James Brennan, Andrew Burton, and Yusuf Lawi, 250–72. East Dar es Salaam, Tanzania: Mkuki na Nyota.

Piertese, Jan Nederveen. 2006. *White on Black: Images of Africa and Blacks in Western Popular Culture*. New Haven: Yale University Press.

Potts, Deborah. 2000. "Urban Unemployment and Migrants in Africa: Evidence from Harare 1985–1994." *Development and Change* 31 (4): 879–910.

Prah, Kwesi. 2002. "Culture, the Missing Link in Development Planning in Africa."

In *Where Has Aid Taken Africa? Rethinking Development,* ed. Kwame Karikari, 33–54. Accra, Ghana: Media Foundation for West Africa.

Rasch, Vibeke. 2003. "Unsafe Abortion in Tanzania: An Empathetic Approach to Improve Post-Abortion Quality of Care." PhD diss., Karolinska Institutel, Stockholm, Sweden.

Rebensdorf, Alicia. n.d. "'Representing the Real': Exploring Appropriations of Hip Hop Culture in the Internet and Nairobi." http://www.lclark.edu/~soan/Alicia/rebensdorf.capital.html (accessed December 4, 2004).

Remes, Peter. 1998. "'Karibu Geto Langu/Welcome in My Ghetto': Urban Youth, Popular Culture and Language in 1990s Tanzania." PhD diss., Northwestern University.

———. 2001. "Global Popular Musics and Changing Awareness of Urban Tanzanian Youth." *Yearbook for Traditional Music* 31:1–26.

Rivoli, Pietra. 2005. "Tanzania: A Second-hand Economy?" Globalist. http://www.theglobalist.com/storyId-aspx?swtoryId=4621.

Roberts, John. 1965. "Kenya's Pop Music." *Transition* 19:40–43.

Rodney, Walter. 1973. *How Europe Underdeveloped Africa.* Dar es Salaam, Tanzania: Tanzania.

Rodrik, Dani. 1997. *Has Globalization Gone Too Far?* Washington, D.C.: Institute for International Economics.

Rofel, Lisa. 1999. *Other Modernities: Gendered Yearnings in China after Socialism.* Berkeley: University of California Press.

Rogo, Khama. 1993. "Induced Abortion in Kenya." Paper prepared for the Center for the Study of Adolescents, International Planned Parenthood Federation, Nairobi, Kenya.

Rose, Tricia. 1994. *Black Noise: Rap Music and Black Culture in Contemporary America.* Middletown, Conn.: Wesleyan University Press.

Ruigrok, Winifred, and Rob Van Tulder. 1995. *The Logic of International Restructuring.* London: Routledge.

Said, Edward. 1980. *Orientalism.* New York: Random.

Samper, David. 2004. "'Africa Is Still Our Mama': Kenyan Rappers, Youth Identity, and the Revitalization of Traditional Values." *African Identities* 2 (1): 37–51.

Schatz, Sayre P. 1992. "The State as Problem and Solution: Predation, Embedded Autonomy, and Structural Change." In *The Politics of Economic Adjustment,* ed. Stephen Haggard and R. R. Kaufman, 98–113. Princeton, N.J.: Princeton University Press.

———. 1994. "Structural Adjustment in Africa: A Failing Grade So Far." *Journal of Modern African Studies* 32 (4): 679–92.

Scott, James. 1985. *Weapons of the Weak: Everyday Forms of Peasant Resistance.* New Haven, Conn.: Yale University Press.

Sewell, William. 1992. "A Theory of Structure: Duality, Agency, and Transformation." *American Journal of Sociology* 98 (1): 1–29.

———. 2005. "The Concept(s) of Culture." In *Practicing History: New Directions in Historical Writing After the Linguistic Turn,* ed. Gabrielle Spiegel, 76–95. New York: Routledge.

Shafer, Leigh A. 2006. "HIV Prevalence and Incidence Are No Longer Falling in Uganda—a Case for Renewed Prevention Efforts: Evidence from a Rural Population Cohort 1989–2005, and from ANC Surveillance." Paper presented at the International AIDS Conference, August 13–18, 2006, Toronto. www.kaisernetwork.org/health_cast/uploaded_files/081706_ias_pc2%25204pm_transcript.pdf (accessed August 22, 2007).

Sharif Hamad. 1993. "AIDS Education Efforts Begin to Address Plight of Tanzania Youth." *AIDS Captions* 1 (1): 20–21.

Shivji, Issa G. 1976. *Class Struggles in Tanzania.* New York: Monthly Review.

———. 2006. *Let the People Speak: Tanzania down the Road to Neo Liberalism.* Dakar, Senegal: CODESRIA.

Singh, Susheela, et al. 2005. "The Incidence of Induced Abortion in Uganda." *International Family Planning Perspectives* 31 (4): 183–91.

Sitas, Ari. 2006. "The African Renaissance Challenge and Sociological Reclamations in the South." *Current Sociology* 54 (3): 357–80.

Spencer, Jonathan. 1996. "Symbolic Anthropology." In *Encyclopedia of Social and Cultural Anthropology,* ed. Alan Barnard and Jonathan Spencer, 535–39. London: Routledge.

Ssewakiryanga, Richard. 1999. "'New Kids on the Block': African-American Music and Uganda Youth." *CODESRIA* 1 and 2:24–28.

———. 2004. "'Bringing the Global Home': Locating Agency in the Reconfiguration of Western Music by Ugandan Youth." In *Sounds of Change: Social and Political Features of Music in Africa,* ed. Stig-Magnus Thorsen, 135–51. Stockholm: Sida Studies.

Steingo, Gavin. 2005. "South African Music after Apartheid: *Kwaito,* the 'Party Politic,' and the Appropriation of Gold as a Sign of Success." *Popular Music and Society* 28 (3): 337–57.

Stiglitz, Joseph. 2003. *Globalization and Its Discontents.* London: Norton.

Stone, Ruth. 2004. *Music in West Africa: Experiencing Music, Expressing Culture.* London: Oxford University Press.

Strange, Susan. 1996. *The Retreat of the State: The Diffusion of Power in the World Economy.* Cambridge, U.K.: Cambridge University Press.

"Strategic Framework, 2007/08." Makerere University, April 2, 2007. www.makerere.ac.ug/makict/documents/strategic_framework/chap3.html (accessed August 13, 2007).

Suggs, David. 2001. *A Bagful of Locusts and the Baboon Woman: Gender, Change, and Continuity in Botswana.* Florence, Ky.: Wadsworth.

Suleyman, Miguel. 2004. "Seventies Music Is All the Rage Again." *East African* May 10, 2004.

Swartz, Sharlene. 2003. "Is Kwaito South African Hip Hop? Why the Answer Matters and Who It Matters To." http://theyouthinstitute.org/pubs/Is%20Kwaito %20South%20African%20Hip%20Hop.pdf (accessed October 11, 2006).

"Tanzanian Anglican Church Still Opposes Condoms, Sex Education." 2006. *Guardian*, August 12, 2006. IPP Media. www.ippmedia.com/ipp/guardian/2006/08/12/72269 .html (accessed July 31, 2007).

Taylor, Ian. 2004. "NEPAD Ignores the Fundamental Politics of Africa." *Contemporary Review* 285 (1662): 29–32.

Tenaille, Frank. 2002. *Music Is the Weapon of the Future: Fifty Years of African Popular Music*. Chicago: Hill.

Tendo, Steve. 2005. "Up-close with Jose Chameleone." www.musicuganda.com, January 20, 2005. http://www.musicuganda.com/chameleone.html (accessed September 10, 2007).

Teng'o, Dan. 2003a. "Wahu Casts a Spell on Music Fans." *Daily Nation* July 12, 2003.

———. 2003b. "Little Substance in New Popular Music." *Daily Nation* July 26, 2003.

Thomas-Slayter, Barbara. 2003. *Southern Exposure: International Development and the Global South in the Twenty-first Century*. Sterling, Va.: Kumarian.

Thompson, Grahame. 1998. "International Competitiveness and Globalization." In *International Competitiveness and Environmental Policies*, ed. T. Baker and J. Kohler, 23–45. Cheltenham, Glasgow, Scotland: Elgar.

Thorsen, Stig-Magnus, ed. 2004. *Sounds of Change: Social and Political Features of Music in Africa*. Stockholm: Swedish International Development Cooperation Agency.

Throup, David. 1993. "Elections and Political Legitimacy in Kenya." *Africa* 63 (3): 371–96.

Throup, David, and Charles Hornsby. 1998. *Multi-Party Politics in Kenya*. London: Currey.

Turner, Victor. 1974. *Dramas, Fields, and Metaphors: Symbolic Action in Human Society*. Ithaca, N.Y.: Cornell University Press.

Ukooflani Mau Mau,. "History." Ukooflani Official Site, October 22, 2006. www .ukooflanimaumau.com/site/en/history.html (accessed January 23, 2007).

"Uganda: Back Condom Use, Museveni Urges Catholic Leaders." 2005. Humanitarian News and Analysis, June 15, 2005. http://www.irinnews.org/Report .aspx?reportid=38692 (accessed July 31, 2007).

UNAIDS. 2006. "UNAIDS/WHO AIDS Epidemic Update: December 2006." www .unaids.org/en/HIV_data/epi2006/default.asp (accessed August 12, 2007).

UNICEF. 2006. "The Report on the Extent and Effect of Sex Tourism and Sexual Exploitation of Children on the Kenyan Coast." www.unicef.de/fileadmin/content_ media/presse/Kenia/report.pdf (accessed January 2, 2007).

Van Binsbergen, Wim. 2004. *Situating Globality: African Agency in the Appropriation of Global Culture*. Leiden, The Netherlands: Brill.

Varnum, John. 1971. "The Obokano of the Gusii: A Bowl Lyre of East Africa." *Ethnomusicology* 15 (2): 242–48.

Wainaina, Binyavanga. 2003. "In Our Own Image." *Sunday Times* (Johannesburg, South Africa), March 23, 2003.

Wakabi, Wairagala. 2006. "Condoms Still Contentious in Uganda's Struggle over AIDS." *Lancet* 367:1387–88.

Walker, Sheila S. 2001. *African Roots/American Cultures: Africa in the Creation of the Americas.* Lanham, Md.: Rowman and Littlefield.

Walker, Sheila, and Jennifer Rasamimanana. 1993. "Tarzan in the Classroom: How 'Educational' Films Mythologize Africa and Miseducate Americans." *Journal of Negro Education* 62 (1): 3–23.

wa Mbugua, Mungai. 2007. "'Is Marwa! It's Ours': Popular Music and Identity Politics in Kenyan Youth Culture." In *Cultural Production and Social Change,* ed. Kimani wa Njogu and G. Oluoch-Olunya, 47–59. Nairobi, Kenya: Twaweza Communications.

Wanambwa, Richard. 2007. "Sex for Marks at Makerere." *Daily Monitor,* July 28, 2007. http://allafrica.com/stories/200707270882.html (accessed August 14, 2007).

wa Njogu, Kimani, and Hervee Mapeau, eds. 2007. *Songs and Politics in Eastern Africa.* Dar es Salaam, Tanzania: Mkuki na Nyota.

Wasserman, Herman, and Sean Jacobs, eds. 2003. *Shifting Selves.* Cape Town, South Africa: Kwela.

Waterman, Christopher. 1990. *Juju: A Social History and Ethnography of an African Popular Music.* Chicago: University of Chicago Press.

———. 1997. "'Our Tradition Is a Very Modern Tradition': Popular Music and the Construction of Pan-Yoruba Identity." In *Readings in African Popular Culture,* ed. Karin Barber, 34–51. London: International African Institute.

wa Thiong'o, Ngugi. 1986. *Decolonising the Mind: The Politics of Language in African Literature.* London: Currey.

Weiss, Brad. 2002. "Thug Realism: Inhabiting Fantasy in Urban Tanzania." *Cultural Anthropology* 17 (1): 93–128.

Weiss, Linda. 1998. *State Capacity: Governing the Economy in a Global Era.* Cambridge, U.K.: Polity.

Wekesa, Peter. 2004. "The Politics of Marginal Forms: Popular Music, Cultural Identity, and Political Opposition in Kenya." *Africa Development,* 29 (4): 92–112.

West, Michael, and William Martin, eds. 1999. *Out of One, Many Africas: Reconstructing the Study and Meaning of Africa.* Urbana: University of Illinois Press.

Widner, Jennifer. 1992. *The Rise of a Party State in Kenya.* Berkeley: University of California Press.

Williams, Cynthia. 1994. "Funders Rethink Priorities: New Era Requires Innovative Approaches to Area and International Studies." *Communique* 4 (2): 1–3.

Wolf, Martin. 2004. *Why Globalization Works.* New Haven, Conn.: Yale University Press.

World Bank. 1981. *Accelerated Development in Sub-Saharan Africa: An Agenda for Action.* Washington, D.C.: World Bank.

———. 1988. *Education in Sub-Saharan Africa: Policies for Adjustment, Revitalization, and Expansion.* Washington, D.C.: World Bank.

———. 1992. *African Development Indicators.* Washington, D.C.: World Bank.

———. 2004. *African Development Indicators.* Washington, D.C.: World Bank.

Xavier, Johnson, and Renalto Rosaldo. 2002. "Introduction: A World in Motion." In *The Anthropology of Globalization: A Reader,* ed. Xavier and Rosaldo, 1–34. Malden, Mass.: Blackwell.

Yambesi, George. 2004. "Rightsizing the Civil Service: The Tanzania Experience of the 1990s." World Bank. www1.worldbank.org/publicsector/civilservice/learning-week2004/presentations/yambesi.ppt (accessed July 21, 2007).

Yarwood, Janette. 2006. "Deterritorialised Blackness: (Re)Making Coloured Identities in South Africa." *Postamble* 2 (1): 46–58.

Zeleza, Paul. 1997. *Manufacturing African Studies and Crises.* Dakar, Senegal: CODESRIA.

Index

MWENDA NTARANGWI is an associate professor of anthropology at Calvin College in Grand Rapids, Michigan. A native of Kenya, Africa, Ntarangwi is the author of *Gender Identity and Performance* and coeditor of *African Anthropologies.*

INTERPRETATIONS OF CULTURE
IN THE NEW MILLENNIUM

Peruvian Street Lives: Culture, Power, and Economy among Market Women
   of Cuzco   *Linda J. Seligmann*
The Napo Runa of Amazonian Ecuador   *Michael Uzendoski*
Made-from-Bone: Trickster Myths, Music, and History from the Amazon
   Jonathan D. Hill
Ritual Encounters: Otavalan Modern and Mythic Community   *Michelle Wibbelsman*
Finding Cholita   *Billie Jean Isbell*
East African Hip Hop: Youth Culture and Globalization   *Mwenda Ntarangwi*

The University of Illinois Press
is a founding member of the
Association of American University Presses.

Composed in 10.5/13 Adobe Minion Pro
by Celia Shapland
at the University of Illinois Press
Manufactured by Cushing-Malloy, Inc.

University of Illinois Press
1325 South Oak Street
Champaign, IL 61820-6903
www.press.uillinois.edu